ALSO BY JEAN LUFKIN BOULER:

Exploring Florida's Emerald Coast
A Rich History and a Rare Ecology

Chasing the Mockingbird
A Memoir of a Broken Mind

THE MOST PERFECT JUSTICE

Alexander McGillivray and George Washington Strive to Save the Creek Nation

By

Jean Lufkin Bouler

Escambia Press

Escambia Press

Birmingham, AL
Contact us: escmbpress@gmail.com

"One of the chiefs gave a brief speech expressing his sense of the honor conferred on the Indians by the kind reception given to them in New York. The mood was festive. The following toasts were drunk:

...

4. May it be the glory of the American empire, to exhibit the most perfect justice towards its Indian allies.

..."

From an account of the welcoming banquet for the Creek delegation, published in the Maryland Journal, *Baltimore, July 30, 1790.*

Author's Note

I have used Creek spelling of rivers and towns, such as Coussa, Ockmulgee and Tallassie. I also used the spelling of the historical period, such as "negociations" and "severalls," when these appear within quotes in order to avoid repeating sic.

The name of the Creek Indians is often spelled Muscogees, but also Muskogees. I chose Muscogees because it is most prevalent.

I have used the term Indians instead of Native Americans because the Creeks likely migrated here from Mexico.

CONTENTS

INTRODUCTION

I became intrigued with Alexander McGillivray while researching a book I was writing about Florida's Emerald Coast, the area between Pensacola and Panama City. While most of the Creek Indians had lived in my home state of Alabama, some had settled in the Florida Panhandle. I learned that McGillivray had been a key player in the history of the new country after the Revolutionary War.

As a former journalist, I sensed a good story that needed to be told. I had grown up in the south Alabama town of Atmore, home to the Poarch tribe that is now the only settlement of the Creeks in their native land. I went to school with Indians and heard my father lament that they had been discriminated against when he was growing up.

For more than 25 years, my husband, Nick, and daughter, Alissa, and I had traveled through the Creek Nation on our five-hour drive from Birmingham to Destin, Florida. I did not realize the historical importance of that area, as well as our Florida destination, to the Creek people.

The references to McGillivray that I came across while researching the Emerald Coast book caught my attention and I knew that I would later pursue that tale. As I began work on this book, I became obsessed with learning more about such an important figure that I, and most Americans, had known nothing about.

I had learned as a young student that Andrew Jackson had driven the Indians off of their lands so Americans could settle there. So, in contrast, I was captivated by the details of how George Washington, his trusted advisor Henry Knox and Creek chief Alexander McGillivray tried to save the Creek Nation after the Revolutionary War. It was a story that I had to write.

Surprisingly, a fair and just Indian policy was the top priority of Washington as the first president of the United States in 1789. He and Knox were adamant that the new country be created as a Federalist government, which should have authority over the states in national matters. They agonized over how to reconcile having American settlers on land that Indians had occupied for centuries. And the Creeks, along with other tribes, had to stake their claim to their lands.

The confrontation between Americans and Indians was at a crisis stage. Washington invited McGillivray to New York to negotiate a treaty that would bring peace and honor to the country that had just fought the English to obtain justice.

Optimism was high as those leaders hammered out an agreement. But in the end, those ideals could not be achieved. I wish I could have written a happier ending.

This book has been an adventure that I hope to share. It is the telling of an important part of our history that has been overlooked. We have rightfully focused on the terrible forced marches of the Indians from their native lands and the repeated, often violent, breaches of treaties over more than 100 years. The efforts of Washington and Knox were a heroic attempt to apply the principles of justice under law and to affirm the highest values of American civic life to our treatment of the Creeks. Those efforts deserve to be remembered.

Knowing the mindset of our post-Revolutionary War heroes gives us much insight into their vision of the country that they had created. Washington and Knox fervently believed that Indians should be treated with the utmost respect and given their entitled place in America. If only that determined stance had survived.

CHAPTER 1

PATH TO POWER

Alexander McGillivray feared that the Creek Nation he led faced destruction. It was 1783, the end of the American Revolutionary War, and he had backed the losing side. He certainly had reason to ponder the fate of his people.

War was nothing new to the Creeks. Battles had long scarred the southeast territory, with the nearby Cherokees fighting British colonists and neighboring Choctaws battling the French. The rival Indians also fought each other over hunting lands. So, those who lived in the southern territory knew life was not always peaceful.

At about the time McGillivray was born, probably in 1759,[1] Europeans vied for control of southern ports. A Creek leader, Chigellie, repeated his father's warning that the English were in the East, the Spanish in the South and the French in the West. "I wish you may not see the Day when they will be for taking your Lands from you, and making Slaves of your Wives and Children," the father lamented.[2]

McGillivray would have to deal with them all. The coming crisis, after the Revolutionary War, would be the greatest peril ever to their lives and land. For generations McGillivray's people had lived on the territory that stretched from what is now Alabama to west Georgia and north Florida, some 62,130 square miles.[3]

But the outcome of the Revolutionary War threatened their very existence. McGillivray had reason to take steps to assure their place in the new country. Some colonists had already settled on Indian soil, then more swarmed into neighboring Georgia onto Creek lands when the Treaty of Paris was signed, ending the war.

McGillivray later would complain that he should have been a party to the treaty talks. Including Indians in negotiations apparently never occurred to any of the officials signing the important document that gave America its freedom, even though the Indians were the ones so affected that they could lose the very place where they had lived for hundreds of years.

White men called these southern Indians Creeks because of the numerous waterways that crisscrossed their land, described by Europeans as beautiful. The landscape occasionally featured mounds of earth about 40 or 50 feet high with a base of some 300 yards across. Creeks at the time of McGillivray did not know who had built the structures.[4]

The Creek Nation was composed of 16 tribes of Muscogees who handed down the story that they had migrated from Mexico in the 1500s when Spanish explorer Hernando de Soto drove them out.[5] They said that the Spanish carried thunder and lightning in their hands.[6] The strong-willed Indians also fought with other tribes along the way from west of the Mississippi and took them into their confederacy. About 15,000 to 20,000 of them lived in towns connected by narrow paths.[7] There were 48 towns in the Upper Creek area along the Tallapoosa, Coosa, and Alabama rivers, in what is now Alabama, and 25 Lower Creek towns on the waters of the Chattahoochee and Flint Rivers in present day Georgia.[8] About 6,000 warriors were available to fight.[9]

The group of Creeks who formed the Lower Creek Towns in Georgia had very different views from the Upper Creeks. Some of the Lower Creeks were settled in Florida. They were called "Seminoles" – meaning runaways by the Spanish or wild men by the Creeks. The Seminoles maintained their independence and land rights, proclaiming their people would protect their territory.[10]

The influx of colonists prompted the Creeks to attack. Towns were designated red for war and white for peace though both would fight. Leaders would debate the merits of resorting to violence.[11] Elders told stories with messages of peace and war to foster negotiation.

"The old Head Men of Note, who being past the fatigue of War and constant Hunting for their Livelyhood, but on Account of the Age held in great Veneration for their Wisdom and Experience, spend the remainder of their days almost intirely in the Town Round Houses, where the Youth and others daily report; relating to them the History of their Nation, discoursing of Occurrences, and delivering precepts and Instructions for their Conduct and Welfare," wrote a British official, Edmond Atkin, in 1755.[12]

Europeans who encountered the Creeks described them as proud, haughty and arrogant yet compassionate, hospitable and generous to strangers they believed would do them no harm. These people were said to be peaceful when unprovoked but quick to resort to violence when confronted by adversaries who threatened them or their lands. Valiant conquerors, they showed mercy to enemies who surrendered and then allowed them into the confederacy.[13] Those characteristics served the Creeks well, enabling them to inhabit their territory for centuries without being driven from their nation.

As far back as the late 1600s, they had to look beyond their undesignated borders to achieve a livelihood. Creeks traded corn and deerskins for horses from the Spanish in Florida missions.[14] In one venture in the 1680s, British traders from Charleston, South Carolina took loads of deerskins carried by 150 Creeks back with them.

Trade was crucial to their way of life and was gained by innovative thinking, which helped them to survive. By 1700 the Creeks were even trading captive Choctaws as slaves for the

English to sell.[15] The Lower Creeks in Florida established a policy of neutrality with the English, Spanish and French for trading.[16] One chief even went to London with Oglethorpe, who founded Georgia in 1732 and had been trading with the Creeks. In a ceremony with King George II, Chief Tomochichi ratified a treaty and was entertained in England for several months.[17] The treaty of 1763 that ended the French and Indian War gave the British control of America east of the Mississippi. This was a good outcome for the Creeks. England protected Indian lands and appointed superintendents to handle matters with them, especially trade.

That relationship with England would benefit both the British and the Creeks, for Indian support in the upcoming Revolutionary War was critical. Which side would the Creeks take? It was an issue that would write history. The chiefs must have agonized over what to do and some in Lower Towns broke from the decision of the majority. The Lower Creek allegiance to the Americans would conflict with the rest of the Creek Nation which developed a relationship with the British and Spanish. That division in town views would lead to important rifts in dealing with Georgians. And paramount to any stand was the effect that it would have on trade, which had become the main economic concern.

The crucial trading path through Alabama and Georgia became known as the Federal Road. Some merchants packed goods into large canoes and navigated waterways to Mobile and New Orleans. Others loaded skins, beeswax, and hickory-nut oil onto packhorses that were small but strong. Each horse carried 180 pounds of goods in three bundles lashed across the saddle and covered with skins to keep dry. A horseman drove 10 horses at a time, using hickory sticks to nudge them forward. The traders drank rum carried in small kegs. They traveled about 25 miles a day, swimming creeks and putting their goods on rafts made of 10-foot canes and dragged by grapevines.[18]

But goods provided by nature were insufficient for changing times. In the decade leading up to the Revolutionary War the Indians had to have weapons and ammunition to fight American intruders. Interestingly, cloth also became a treasured item that they would gladly barter for their deerskins. The Indians preferred wool or cotton cloth rather than leather or fur.

Over the years, a complex network of trade with Europeans partially replaced the ages-old tradition of hunting. Unfortunately, the Creeks became so dependent on trade that they went into debt with the British and Spanish and some could only pay by giving up land.[19] Trade goods became increasingly important to the tribes who previously had not acquired possessions.

"In former times, we were entirely unacquainted with the customs of the white people, but since they have come among us, we have been clothed as they are, and accustomed to their ways, which makes it at this day absolutely necessary that we should be supplied with goods," said Creek leader Mortar.[20]

Some of the town chiefs became wealthy from gifts and bribes, to the dismay of their people. A colonist noted that Tomochichi drew criticism from his fellow townspeople.

"They say he has Sold them to the English for the presents he has received and what he tells them of the Grandeur & People of our Nation is a Lye to keep them in Awe, and indeed I must Say I could wish Tomochichi and his Wife would Communicate some of us Presents to his People," wrote colonist Thomas Christie.[21]

The traders were clever enough to figure a way to gain favor in the Creek Nation. They often married Creek women of prestigious clans to get in the good graces of town chiefs, called micos. So there were a number of children who were half Creek and half European.[22]

In this economy that was central to Creek existence, most towns had a white trader. One who quickly learned the value of Indian commerce was Lachlan McGillivray, Alexander's father. The young red-haired Lachlan had sailed from Dunmaglass Scotland to Charleston around 1738.[23] He was only 16 years old and had very little money in his pocket. However, his extended family had been traders and the profession would become his calling as well.[24]

He was astute and eager to begin a new life in America. He was not afraid of Indians. In Charleston he met up with traders who were going to carry goods to Creek country. Lachlan realized it was a good opportunity and joined them. He had "an honest heart, a fearless disposition, and cheerful spirits, which seldom became depressed."[25] Part of Lachlan's pay was a jack knife. He traded it to an Indian for deerskins, then, back in Charleston sold the skins. It was the beginning of what would become a very profitable venture for the young man who was eager to learn the business and develop a friendly relationship with the Creeks.[26]

Lachlan moved in 1745 to the heart of Creek country, Little Tallassie, meaning village of the walnut trees, on a bluff near present day Montgomery, Alabama, to operate a trading post. The village, one of the largest in the Creek Nation, stood on a plain surrounded by small hills near the Tallapoosa River. A public building where ceremonies and business were conducted dominated a central square. Other structures stored deerskins and corn. One pavilion was used for cooking and another for lounging. Houses made of tree limbs and clay plaster walls decorated with hieroglyphics provided family lodging and storage of grain and potatoes surrounding the center of town. The Indians planted vegetables in one big field that was marked off for each family. Some of the crops were put into a public storage area for the mico to distribute as he wished to other towns, to travelers or for expeditions.[27]

Lachlan became immersed in the Creek culture. He learned the Muskogean language and even served as an interpreter in dealings between the Creeks and Europeans.[28] Chiefs came to his house and he went to their councils and ball games.

At that time, the Creeks did not have a central chief. "…there is no coercive power in any of their nations, their kings can do no more than to persuade," wrote Georgia founder Oglethorpe. "All the power they had is no more than to call their old men and captains together and to propound to them the measures they think proper; and after they have done speaking, all the others have liberty to give their opinions also; and they reason together with great temper and modesty till they have brought each other into some unanimous resolution."[29]

Called humane and intelligent, Lachlan was also known to be trustworthy. He was instrumental in bringing peace between the Creeks and Cherokees because the Indians viewed him as steady and honest.[30]

The young Scot met a Creek woman, Sehoy Marchand, whose father was a French officer later killed during a mutiny. Her mother was a Creek aristocrat from the Wind Clan, the most powerful. The Creeks traced their ancestry through their mothers who belonged to various clans. Nine clans, named for mythical ancestors, of Creek mothers' lineage formed the social and political hierarchy of the nation. Children belonged to the mother's clan.[31]

In order to abide by Creek tradition, Lachlan likely would have courted Sehoy by sending gifts to her through a proxy. If she was in favor of marrying him, the proxy would then ask for the consent of the young woman's maternal relatives and members of the clan for their consent.[32]

According to family lore, Sehoy dreamed of books, pen and ink while she was pregnant with Alexander, a prophesy of his becoming a scholar. He was born and given the name of Hoboi-Hili-Miko, the Good Child King.[33]

Lachlan built a house at Hickory Ground near Little Tallassie and planted an apple orchard. Lachlan lived there for 12 years before moving to Georgia where he owned trading stores in Augusta and Savannah. He became wealthy trading deerskin leather for British wool. He amassed 11,000 acres of land, where he farmed and raised livestock on two plantations with the help of slaves.[34]

It was the custom of Creeks for the mother to make decisions about their children. Lachlan convinced his wife to let Alexander go to Charleston to live with a relative, Farquhar McGillivray, and be tutored by the scholars George Sheed and William Henderson. The young boy received a classical education, studying European history, Latin and learning to speak English and Spanish. Those lessons would play a major role in his diplomatic approach to Creek leadership in the future. At the age of 17, he went to Savannah, living on his father's plantation.[35] He apprenticed at a trading company that was a large slave-trading operation.[36]

Lachlan became quite prominent and political. Gifted as a trader and a businessman, he became one of the most successful merchants in America.[37] His reputation for fairness led to his being named justice of the peace. Later he was appointed commissioner of security and defense and was an intermediary between the Creeks and English. The Georgia Assembly honored him a number of times for his help with Indian affairs. He was elected to the assembly and counseled the new Governor James Wright on the Creeks and Choctaws who were at war battling over hunting grounds.[38]

When American colonists revolted against England in 1775 Lachlan became a loyalist because if the colonists won the war, they might want even more land. In fact, Georgia confiscated his Savannah plantation and other properties worth more than $100,000, a fortune at the time.[39] He moved back to Scotland in 1782.[40]

Alexander had returned to Hickory Ground in Creek country by 1777. That Creek world was very different from the one where he had become educated. But Alexander McGillivray had no trouble making the adjustment from one way of life to the other. He was well educated, quick minded and desirous of leading his people. He was well aware of his place in Creek society. He wrote as a young man that the powerful Wind Clan that he descended from would allow him to have significant influence in the Creek Nation.[41]

Just as important, he was given a commission by the British to build a relationship between England and the Upper Creeks. That post, along with his Wind Clan background, gave him a powerful voice in Creek matters. Town councils were well represented by Wind Clan members and were inclined to listen to McGillivray.[42] They called him *Isti alcagagi thlucco,* Great Beloved Man.[43]

McGillivray was lighter skinned than his fellow tribesmen, who were of copper-red color, since his father was a Scot and his mother was half French. Like his fellow Creeks, he was tall and slender with a handsome face and broad forehead. His hair was pulled back.[44] His mixed race was not unusual as other white traders who lived in Creek country fathered children with Indian women. Some 600 whites had settled in Creek towns during that period which meant a significant population of mixed-race offspring.[45]

McGillivray followed the Creek practice of allowing more than one wife and had a second one at a home he owned on Little

River in Baldwin County in south Alabama. Little has been recorded about her. His primary residence was at Hickory Ground where his father had lived.[46] His house was more like those of white men than Indians. It was a log structure with dormer windows and a stone fireplace. Some 60 black slaves worked on the property, which still had a couple of apple orchards, hogs and cattle.[47] Cabins for the slaves gave the plantation the appearance of a small village.[48]

The Creeks had taken in fugitive black slaves who had escaped from colonists, treating them almost as equals. But when the deerskin market declined, some Creeks turned to trading black slaves as a way to get goods they had become accustomed to, such as wool, guns and rum.[49]

The people McGillivray saw every day were dressed very differently from those he had encountered in Charleston and Savannah. Men in Little Tallassie wore headbands decorated with beads or a plume of feathers. They dressed in ruffled shirts and a flap pulled through a belt over their loins. Leggings and moccasins with a cloak of fine cloth completed their attire. The women were said to be beautiful with large, black eyes, high cheekbones and high forehead. They wore skirts and a decorated blouse. Their raven-black hair was plaited.[50] Both men and women decorated their bodies with feathers and wore stone, bead or silver necklaces. They punctured their skin and rubbed in dye to make tattoos of the moon, animals or other designs.[51]

McGillivray likely combined the attire of white men and Indians for himself, taking advantage of cloth that was traded to the Creeks. He would have wanted his Creek people to think of him as one of their own. When he negotiated with Spanish and British officials, on the other hand, he would have worn clothes that put him on an equal footing. For at least one special occasion he was described as wearing a suit like that of the Europeans or colonists.

The Creek Nation was frequently traveled by Indians themselves and by European traders. Trails through Creek country were 18 to 24 inches wide, just enough for a horse and rider. Some were on ridges, others along rivers and creeks. Notches in tree bark indicated various messages, such as direction to a destination or warning to trespassers.[52] The Indians made log rafts or built footbridges across waterways.

For their livelihood, natural resources were in abundance. Creeks, streams, rivers and lakes provided sturgeon, trout, perch, rockfish and red drum. Women usually did the fishing in spring and summer with spears, poison or nets. Deer and bear roamed forests of oak, hickory and chestnut, providing meat as well as skins. Forests yielded wood for fires, but the Creeks did not cut down the trees. Instead, women gathered fallen limbs and branches. Some hardwood trees grew to 11 feet in trunk diameter, with branches spanning 100 feet. Stands of pine also spread over the landscape.[53]

Women kept a low fire burning in their house yards, where they usually had food cooking throughout the day."[54] In the fall, several inches of hickory nuts covered the ground and were gathered by women to make into oil for cooking for the year. The fertile soil in many areas and mild climate produced corn, beans, potatoes and other staples as well as melons, strawberries, peaches and apples.[55] Small plots at each house yielded fruits and vegetables owned by that family. But large communal fields outside of town that women tended were the property of the village.[56]

Communication by most of the Creeks was face-to-face since they could not read or write. McGillivray was in a unique position of being able to correspond with Spanish and British officials by letter. He was constantly writing to them asking for advice or letting them know of developments in his nation. Runners who could travel 25 miles a day carried his messages to

Pensacola, Mobile, New Orleans and occasionally St. Augustine. Much of McGillivray's interaction with the Europeans would deal with commerce. Trade became the backbone of their economy and the Creeks had to have an agent to represent them.[57]

Creek tribes were becoming unified under the prominent leader Emistisiguo, also of Little Tallassie.[58] So, McGillivray lived in the center of power where many decisions were made about the Creeks. Councils of the chief, elderly Creeks and warriors also were held there.[59] No doubt McGillivray was a respected voice in political matters.[60]

In the evening, the village people socialized. After work in the fields they gathered for entertainment in the form of dances, games and drinking.[61] Music was made with cane flutes, gourd rattles and skin drums played to songs and chants.[62]

Medicine men treated illnesses with willow bark which was soaked and used as a tonic for fevers. The mixture had ingredients similar to aspirin. Many herbs, such as sassafras and cherry bark were also used for cures. Since some illnesses were believed to be caused by animals, the medicine men used magic along with the plants for healing.

A strong black drink was consumed as part of their ritual of meetings or welcoming friendly visitors. Yupon leaves were browned in a large clay pot, then brought to boiling. When cooled, the mixture was poured into a gourd with a hole in it and passed around the central house at the square. They vomited after several drinks to purify their stomachs, and then smoked a pipe. The ceremony was a way of uniting the men of the town and welcoming visitors.[63] It was a symbol of cleansing and peace.

The ritual must have seemed odd to McGillivray after living in the white man's world. But he would have been familiar with the custom as a child and certainly would have felt obligated to participate as a Creek leader.

A few years before McGillivray came home, William Bartram, an American naturalist, traveled through Creek country using deerskin traders as his guides and wrote about what he saw. He noted that alcohol was the big evil. Some Indians had tried to curtail it. Two traders he met had a haul of kegs that they were about to drink when the vessels were hacked open by Creek raiders and spilled.[64] McGillivray himself was said to be a heavy drinker, but it is not known whether his alcohol consumption caused some of the debilitating illnesses that he would develop.

In a ceremony that was entirely different from his school days in Charleston, McGillivray would have participated in the most important rite, the annual Green Corn Ceremony, called busk, celebrating harvest.

Busk occurred around the first of August. The Indians built a new central fire and burned old clothes and household items in a big heap. The priest tossed in several pieces of corn with a piece of meat while he prayed. Boys took flaming wood from the fire to each house, which had been cleansed. The limbs were kept burning for four days while warriors danced and bathed in the river. Women had to stay away for a while and then were purified with willow roots.[65]

The young danced for entertainment wearing their finest clothes and painting their bodies. Men and women danced separately, in a circular motion, sometimes in single file and sometimes in twos. They also played ball games similar to lacrosse. Teams of about a dozen tried to get a ball between goals by passing it using web-like sticks. Older men played lawn bowling or gambled using different size sticks or different colors of beans.[66]

A few months later, the focus of these tribesmen was on hunting, the main staple of goods and skins to be traded. Hunting season was from November to February. Towns were mostly deserted as everyone except the very young and very old went to the woods.[67] Men stalked deer with guns or bows in winter, up to 30 miles a day by foot. Tokens of thanks were given when deer were slain by burying a bead or tossing a chunk of meat into a fire. Hunters carried Physic-nut, or Indian olive, with them when tracking deer because they thought it lured the prey to them.[68] McGillivray did not participate in hunts. In the winter, he went to the coast near his Little River plantation to live among Spaniards.[69]

Always using natural resources, hickory nuts were stored, as many as 100 bushels for one family. After pounding the nut, they were boiled and put through strainers to get sweet rich cream to put in hominy and corn cakes.[70] Days were also spent by women making pottery, moccasins and decorative clothing. Their traditions were well recorded. When someone died, families buried the dead in a sitting position with prized possessions under the cabin where they lived.[71]

McGillivray was much aware of how the Creek Nation functioned with its social and governmental hierarchy. Each village had a mico, who presided over town meetings, as well as a war chief and a high priest. The high priest, believed to commune with spirits, had a lot of say in military matters because the spirits he was linked to could predict the outcome of battle. The priests even sometimes stopped war parties on the day before battle.[72]

But while McGillivray was away becoming educated, his homeland began undergoing cultural changes that affected the essence of tribal life. Young warriors engaged in raids against white settlers that were not approved by headsmen. One Creek leader said he took great pains to rule his young people.[73]

Disagreement developed between young and old in debating the views of red and white towns. Even mothers feared that their offspring were overstepping bounds in threatening to kill colonists.[74] The elders who had told stories were saddened that few came to hear them. Disease killed many of the older Creeks, leaving a gap in the generational exchange of ideas.[75]

CHAPTER 2

ESCALATING TENSIONS

The Creeks would face even more challenges during the Revolutionary War. Who should they support? Neutrality was an option that would avoid pitting them against either side. But trade hinged on loyalty and if hindered, hunters and warriors would not have weapons and there would be no one to buy their deerskins. Without an ally the Creeks would just be left dangling on their own, without goods or protection.[76]

In 1774, in an effort to persuade the Creeks to side with them, the British named mapmaker and surveyor David Taitt as their agent. He settled in Little Tallassie, the political center where Chief Emistisiguo and the influential McGillivray lived, home of the powerful Wind Clan. "There he soon became acquainted with the most gifted and remarkable man that ever was born upon the soil of Alabama," noted historian Albert James Pickett wrote, referring to McGillivray.[77] McGillivray took a liking to Taitt who became engrossed in Creek customs and even married McGillivray's cousin.

Taitt was able to marshal the Upper Creeks to help British forces fight the colonists.[78] He convinced the Indians that the Americans were blocking trade in Savannah and Charleston and stealing ammunition intended for the Creeks from the king of England.[79]

However, the Lower Creeks, in south Georgia and north Florida, were more sympathetic to the Americans and tried to kill Taitt. He, however, escaped to Pensacola, which was occupied by the Spanish. That difference in loyalty split the

Creek Nation. The two regions strongly upheld their separate alliances. One Lower Creek chief even threatened to kill McGillivray.[80] And McGillivray thwarted a plot and saved Emistisiguo from being assassinated by the opposing faction.[81]

Emistesigo threw his support to the British in hopes that they would protect Indian lands from encroachment by American colonists. And he was willing to take his beliefs to the battlefield. His leadership surely influenced McGillivray who also would side with England. But the stand of the Lower Creeks with the Americans thwarted McGillivray's attempt to unify a council of chiefs that met annually. The group decided to remain neutral. Yet, some towns maintained their independence and followed McGillivray in backing the British.[82]

Creek leaders would face yet another problem as colonial settlers and traders brought cattle into the area. The cows devastated the deer and bear populations by destroying grasses and other natural vegetation. Those destructive herds threatened the very livelihood of the Indians. Emistesigo and other Creeks appealed to Georgia Governor Jame Wright, quoting Lachlan McGillivray as saying that cattle should not go beyond your yards. Since the admired trader had come to Creek country as a young man, he knew well how they lived and that white people should be satisfied with Indian food rather than substituting cow for venison, Emistesigo said.[83]

Other countries were also embedded in Creek territory. For the Spanish, British and French, Creek country was a prime region in the New World. And McGillivray had to figure out a way to keep them all satisfied.

One European who became immersed in Creek life and was very influential was a French officer, Le Clerc Milfort. In May of 1776 at a council meeting in the town of Coetas McGillivray met him. At the square where the assembly met were 12 cabins where some 40 to 60 men slept. Most of the huts were painted red, except for three facing the setting sun, which were painted white as a symbol of virtue and old age and were decorated with garlands of flowers. These cabins were for elderly men who were highly regarded and respected. In time of war the red cabins had a chain of wood rings that informed warriors to be prepared for battle. In peace, there were garlands of ivy. The cabin of the grand chief faced the rising sun to indicate that he must always watch over the interest of the nation. Next to it was the main building where the assemblies were held.[84]

McGillivray sat in the center of the meeting on a bearskin rug. He did not speak French so he and Milfort conversed in English, which McGillivray spoke very well and Milfort spoke haltingly. Milfort knew of McGillivray from American and British newspaper articles. He came to Creek country on a mission to befriend these important tribes so that France could be counted as an ally. He was hugely successful.

His entry into their culture began, as was the custom, with black drink. Gourds of the traditional mixture were passed around. The men vomited the drink to make sure everyone had a stomach free of food and alcohol, that they were too fond of and that could influence decisions.[85] An orator stood in front of Milfort and spoke for nearly an hour.

Afterwards, old men stood in a line, marched past him, shook his hand and gave him tobacco in a pouch made of swanskin. It was white as a sign of peace and friendship. With a meal of roast meat such as fowl, deer, beef or turkey and bread, they enjoyed sagamite, a drink made from boiling corn meal that tasted like cider.[86]

Since he was a visitor, Milfort was asked to leave before the assembly business got underway. McGillivray presided.[87]

After the council, Milfort joined McGillivray for a meal at an elderly man's house. Then, McGillivray invited him to go to his home at Little Tallassie. The journey took four days. "Near this village, and on Coussa River, is the house that McGillivray lived in," Milfort wrote. It was about two miles from Fort Toulouse, formerly occupied by the French. "This plantation seemed beautiful to me," he observed.[88]

Milfort described McGillivray as having "mildness of manners" and a respectable reputation that defied the negative opinion that the Anglo-Americans had of him.[89]

McGillivray invited Milfort to live in one of his houses. "One will not be astonished that this bond was so quickly established, when one is informed that McGillivray, although born in the midst of a savage nation, was far from being uncivilized himself, and had much knowledge and intelligence," Milfort wrote. He noted that McGillivray's father, who was a Scot, had taught him only the English language; so that he spoke very poorly that of the people among whom he lived and of whom he had become one of the chiefs. What made learning the Creek language difficult for him was the fact that there were 10 to 12 different languages among the tribes that had been brought into the Creek Nation.

McGillivray enjoyed Milfort's company because he could learn about the manners and habits of Europeans. His interests and demeanor made him a valuable diplomat to Milfort and others who sought his support. He was a scholarly Creek who could command the respect of his tribes as well as European officials.

Milfort, as other Europeans before him, found that he was much impressed by McGillivray's sincerity and civilized way of life. He accepted McGillivray's invitation to live at Hickory Ground and became part of the Indian community. Although he referred to them as savages, he said he had never encountered people as grateful and generous.[90] Old chiefs told him how belts of small seeds told the history of their people.[91]

After a number of requests from Milfort, McGillivray allowed him to become a soldier. Whites and certain Indian tribes were making frequent raids in Creek lands. The chiefs called a council of war to decide on a plan of attack. They asked Milfort for advice but retained their war traditions, which were elaborate.

A chain of wooden rings was put on a red cabin to inform warriors to be prepared for battle.[92] The head war chief then sent a red club to each town with a number of sticks to indicate how many days until warriors would gather at a meeting place. Each day at dawn a stick was thrown away until the day of the last one. Stakes marked an area to show how many warriors were needed to fill the space and go to fight. They drank war medicine for three days that would purge infection from battle wounds.[93]

The warriors fought naked to keep bits of clothing from getting into wounds, causing infection. They painted their bodies in many colors and looked "more frightful than the devils which appear in the opera ballets," Milfort observed.[94] In battle, warriors walked in single file, led by a chief, as they approached the enemy so the opposing force couldn't tell how many fighters they were facing. Scouts in front and to the rear prevented surprise attacks. When they stopped, they sat in a circle with legs crossed, guns by their sides. The chief signaled when it was time to sleep and to awake. Sentinels watched over them.[95]

However, they adopted Milfort's battle tactics. A dramatic change from Creek tradition was that the warriors began to make surprise attacks at night. Milfort also convinced them to take up strategic positions that would shield them from the enemy. As they approached the enemy, their strategy for battle was successful. Milfort kept winning.[96]

In battle, the warriors scalped their dead enemies. Milfort wrote that when a young man took his first scalp, he earned a war name instead of that given by his mother and became eligible to pursue marriage.[97]

McGillivray, despite his leadership skills, was not a great warrior. Milfort told a story of the great leader hiding naked in the bushes during a skirmish with colonists and taking a slain man's clothing afterward. He said he and McGillivray later laughed about the episode.

"When one has as much administrative knowledge and as noble a heart as Alexander McGillivray had, one does not need military abilities to be a great man," Milfort wrote in his journal.[98]

Numerous battles against the Americans prompted all the Creek town chiefs to hold a grand council in May of 1780. In January of that year, Georgia had passed a so-called headright law which granted every white male who was head of a household 200 acres of land, plus another 50 acres for each dependent, up to 1,000 acres. That legislation was a bonanza for white settlers. But disastrous for Indians. The land in question was Creek territory.[99]

As if that was not enough, additional grants were given to Revolutionary veterans, which further fueled the fury over land. Some 2,000 soldiers who had served were given about 750,000 acres in Georgia. Some even came from other states and took advantage of their grants.[100]

The Treaty of Paris further eroded the Creek Nation by transferring territory claimed by Great Britain West of the Appalachians and East of the Mississippi to the United States, and returning Florida to Spain. Tensions escalated as the colonists claimed the land as their own. Georgia was especially aggressive. Prime land was between the Ogeechee and Oconee rivers, a region the Creeks had long deemed valuable. Georgia desperately wanted to establish settlements there but did not have enough power to go to war over it and could not convince the United States to fight with them.[101]

McGillivray was outraged that Britain gave away his people's territory. "…She has no right to give up a Country she never coud call her own," he wrote to Spanish official Estavan Miro.[102]

At the Creek grand council in 1780, the chiefs were to pick a war chief. During such grand assemblies no one could leave until all of the business had been completed. At night they would sleep in cabins in the town square or in the grand cabin. A drum called them back in the morning.[103]

In a complex three-day ceremony, the assembled chiefs offered the head military position to McGillivray. But he declined because of poor health and, according to Milfort, "was not very fond of fighting."[104]

McGillivray suggested Milfort. The Frenchman said he could not accept a position that would put him over McGillivray, so the chiefs voted to make McGillivray supreme chief of the Creek Nation. "He was thereby entrusted with all the political and administrative affairs of the nation and I with all the military affairs," Milfort wrote.[105]

Warriors carried Milfort on a litter covered with a bearskin draped with garlands of ivy to the grand cabin. They whooped and danced in the procession, holding eagle tails on sticks. Medicine men made a tea drink called war medicine. They all vomited as they drank. Swan wings were passed over chiefs' faces. Then, they sweated in steam made from boiling water poured over pebbles in a fire followed by plunging into the cold river. After a feast, the procession took Milfort back to his house where the oldest mico proclaimed him war chief. He must endure cold, heat and hunger to defend the nation.

Milfort and his warriors were successful. Newspapers gave credit to McGillivray. One article said, "With what skill he directs this unfortunate war against us; if it were possible to win him over and have him to act in our interest, we would be fortunate, because the other Indians would no longer dare make war on us; let us try to make peace with him." Milfort and

McGillivray were amused by the accounts. McGillivray "was spending his time very quietly at home," Milfort wrote.[106]

The Creeks continued to aid the British in battle. In 1782, at Savannah, Emistesigo and his warriors fought against Americans who were trying to take the town from British forces. He was killed.[107]

Milfort urged Cherokee and other tribes to quit fighting each other and unite against the patriots. In 1785, a Grand War Council was created that would meet in Creek territory every year and plan strategy.[108]

Later, Milfort decided to leave the Creek Nation when France became allied with the colonists. He didn't want to be in the position of fighting his own country. His service to the Creeks had been crucial at a time of crisis. In his journal, he might have exaggerated his importance at times, according to some historians, but his first-hand observation of Creek country and McGillivray revealed an intimate look at their customs and beliefs.

CHAPTER 3

"CONTINENT IN CONFUSION"

After Emistisiguo was killed in battle, McGillivray succeeded him as sole leader after being named supreme chief by the grand council. Chiefs in Florida would later go against his wishes. But McGillivray himself certainly assumed the role of head of the Creek Nation in his dealings with England, Spain and the United States. And those countries considered him chief negotiator for the Creeks.

Since McGillivray had not grown up in Creek country and was not fluent in the Muscogee, he used an interpreter when talking with fellow Creeks. Still, he thought of himself as a Creek. In a letter to Panton, he said, "we Indian country folks," and to Georgia officials he said settlers were depriving "us" of land that was necessary for "our Subsistence." To U.S. commissioners, he referred to himself as "a native and ruling chief…very deeply interested in the fate of my country."[109]

McGillivray ambitiously took risks with high stakes negotiations. If those talks and agreements were successful, his lands would be protected; failure could lead to the demise of the Creek Nation. His instincts turned out to be very good for his people.

The new chief embraced the Creek Nation with courage and an unfailing ability to negotiate for its survival. His classical education in Latin and Greek as well as his knowledge of British and European history served him well as a diplomat. McGillivray was able to negotiate because he was fluent in Spanish and English.[110]

Like Emistisiguo, he continued to side with the British, who made him a colonel with pay. He was likely influenced by his close relationship with British agent Taitt and resented the colonists taking his father's property in Georgia.

He presided over micos from each town at the regional council in May every year. They remained there for several days and nights. Women brought food and drink but could go no closer than 20 paces. A fire burned continuously, and young men danced around it at sunset.

McGillivray had to deal with the conflict between Spain and Great Britain vying for control of the southern coast as well as the invasion of colonists to the east in Georgia and north in Tennessee. The Paris Treaty of 1783 that ended the Revolutionary War included the provision granting Spain East and West Florida although England would later contest the boundary.[111]

"The whole Continent is in Confusion," McGillivray wrote to Arturo O'Neill, the Spanish governor of West Florida. "Before long I expect to hear that the three kings (of England, Spain, and France) must settle the matter by dividing America between them."[112]

The fate of the Creek Nation depended on McGillivray's ability to juggle the varying interests. His importance became widely known.

"…I am well informed" that McGillivray "has more influence among the Creek Nations than any other person," O'Neill wrote in a 1783 letter to another Spanish official.[113]

The Spanish wanted to befriend the Creeks to keep Americans from settling in their region. In an important move, William Panton, who knew McGillivray's father, built the most powerful trade house in the area, Panton, Leslie & Company. He introduced McGillivray to Spanish authorities in Pensacola and New Orleans and brought him in as a partner. McGillivray hoped Spain would prevent Americans from encroaching on

Creek lands and Spain saw Creek country as a buffer between them and Americans.

The stream of colonists settling in Georgia created an escalating crisis that could not be ignored. Land was precious. Surprisingly, the issue continued to split the unity of the Creeks as some Lower Towns supported the Americans. In a bold move, two chiefs, Tame King of the Upper Town of Tallassee and Fat King of the Lower Creek town of Cusseta, went to Augusta in November 1783, and agreed with Georgia commissioners to cede a huge swath of land between the Ogeechee and Oconee rivers. In return, their debts to traders would be paid and commerce would start anew.[114]

The price demanded by Georgia was three million acres, which the state claimed was compensation for the Creeks siding with the British during the Revolutionary War. Since the British could no longer restrain expansion, Georgia was determined to take much of the territory.[115]

McGillivray was appalled and did not honor the treaty, declaring that it did not represent the will of the Creek Nation. The agreement would set a precedent of willingness to give up territory that had long belonged only to the Creeks. And so, the Upper and Lower sections became even more bitterly divided. The land in dispute was already surveyed and settled so McGillivray's warriors attacked and killed many of the colonists living there.[116] If Creeks adhered to the treaty, they would give up much of their territory and open the door for even more white settlements with no end in sight.

McGillivray turned to the Spanish. He wrote to them that Georgia wanted to establish trade, but that he would refrain from attacking Spanish outposts if they would help protect Creek lands. In return, they would receive a barrier to thwart Americans from encroaching on Spanish territory. In addition, he demanded a trade guarantee so that Spain would supply needed goods rather than the Creeks having to rely on Georgia traders.[117]

A few months after the Treaty of Augusta, McGillivray and a few Creek leaders went to Pensacola and signed a treaty of alliance with Spain. The agreement protected Creek lands within Spanish territory and guaranteed an all-important trade network. The Creeks promised not to trade with Americans and would turn over anyone trying to rebel against Spain.[118]

Spain also agreed to provide goods and avoid encroaching on Creek lands.[119] The Spanish appointed McGillivray commissary for the Creeks with the rank and pay of colonel at a salary of $600 a year, what a Creek hunter would earn over 25 years.[120] Esteban Miro, governor of Louisiana, wrote that Spain wanted McGillivray to be commissary of the Creek Nation because of his "well-known good disposition, zeal, and affection…promoting by every possible means the honor, glory, and reciprocal interest of both nations."[121]

The Panton, Leslie and Company trading firm was authorized to operate in Pensacola, and McGillivray would be a silent partner.[122] Over a period of more than a year McGillivray had negotiated with the Spanish while Panton gained a monopoly of trade with the Creeks.[123] The Creeks could get goods from Panton, Leslie only by having a requisition signed by McGillivray.[124] Panton became indebted to McGillivray because the Creek trade made him a rich man. His main store in Pensacola stocked goods valued at $50,000 and employed 15 clerks. Valuable skins and furs were sorted in skin houses and packed for foreign markets. He owned 15 schooners to ship them.[125]

McGillivray became the most powerful figure in the Creek Nation because all traders had to have a license from him, and he had gifts and goods distributed to towns. The amount of goods was not trivial. For example, one transaction included 300 pounds of gunpowder, 600 pounds of shot and 200 flints. McGillivray himself gave out treasured items. One day he handed out a couple of dozen shirts and three dozen knives. Just a few days later, he distributed more provisions to 420 fellow tribesmen at Little Tallassee. His powerful role in trade earned him the title of "most beloved man."[126]

The Pensacola Treaty was especially significant because in addition to giving McGillivray control of trade, it established his role as leader and chief negotiator for the Creek Nation, even though councils still made decisions. Tame King and Fat King continued to oppose him.[127] McGillivray resorted to armed warriors to protect him against Georgians and to assassinate several white supporters of his Creek opponents. He seized Tame King's house, crops and livestock.[128] Yet, McGillivray fervently believed the Creeks could only be successful in saving themselves if they were unified as a powerful entity rather than adhering to the tradition of town autonomy. The impressive number of up to 6,000 warriors, many more than the Spanish or Americans could call to arms, made him a strong voice to be reckoned with.[129]

McGillivray further sealed his relationship with Spain in numerous letters to Miro and O'Neill. In one 1784 letter, he complained to O'Neill that supplies were insufficient for one town much less the entire Creek Nation and asked for more goods so the Creeks would not be dependent on Americans for trade. The British had provided protection but were leaving St. Augustine, he said, which meant the Creeks would need more arms to defend themselves.[130]

When border wars erupted between the Creeks and Georgia, the Spanish supplied weapons because they wanted to monopolize Creek trade.[131] Even though McGillivray did not engage in battle himself he frequently sent warriors on raids. And he did not hesitate to use violence when settlers invaded his land.

He executed a white officer and two others in a public square because they had opposed him. "Public examples are sometimes necessary particularly in this country, as executing one notorious offender, oftentimes saves the lives of severalls, as the Indians themselves in such cases observes no bounds," McGillivray wrote.[132]

Within the Creek Nation, McGillivray did not hesitate to maintain power by being the authority who controlled trade. Towns had Panton, Leslie and Company traders who also could only do business with a license from McGillivray. While doling out arms, ammunition and other gifts from the King of Spain to allies he neglected his enemy Creek chiefs.[133]

The standoff between McGillivray and the Georgians threatened to explode. In New York, the new American government would have to decide what role, if any, the federal officials should have in determining Indian policy. A central concern was who would have the authority to act. Congress passed a law giving itself the right to manage Indian affairs and created north and south departments to report to the Secretary of War, but also said states rights should not be violated. And the new U.S. Constitution authorized Congress to regulate commerce with Indians.[134]

However, Georgia strongly believed that it had the right to negotiate treaties and control land in its own state. The question of federalism versus states rights would not diminish.

In 1785, as something of a compromise, Congress appointed commissioners to negotiate with the Creeks. They wrote a letter to McGillivray asking him to meet their agents and negotiate an agreement. McGillivray wrote back on September 5, 1785, from Little Tallassie and agreed to meet with the Americans to settle matters on an equitable footing. He said he was surprised that it had taken so long for the United States government to take steps to resolve differences between the new states and the Creeks. He said the Georgians had not treated Indians fairly and that the Spanish had been Creek protectors. He would use any angle, especially the Spanish, to support his stand.

McGillivray wrote that he and his people only wanted justice and protection of their hunting grounds. "They had been ours from the beginning of time, and I trust that, with the assistance of our friends, we shall be able to maintain them against every attempt that may be made to take them from us," he wrote. Appeals to Georgians had gone unheard, he complained.[135]

McGillivray told O'Neill of the American request in a letter and assured him that the Creeks would remain loyal to Spain. McGillivray confessed that he had faults but these did not include deceit and treason and that he definitely did not want to have his actions, of a generous mind, be watched with suspicion and distrust.

He noted that his nation engaged in a treaty of alliance and friendship with Spain because they could be of mutual advantage to each other. The Creeks would be an asset to the King's interest and assure Spain that they would not trade with any other power.

"I have only to add that Your Excellency may be assured that I shall give You the earliest Information how the Indians & the Americans have Settled the grand dispute in question about Lands, & any other Matters that comes to my knowledge in the course of this Negotiation," he wrote.[136] O'Neill advised McGillivray not to treat with the Americans.

But McGillivray thought differently. He hoped that good results would come from dealing directly with the federal officials. And he had little choice. Any step toward bringing about peace and fending for his land had to be pursued. He wrote to United States Indian commissioner Andrew Pickens that he would be pleased to attend a treaty conference. He also said he was optimistic that the commissioners and Creeks could reach an equitable agreement. McGillivray criticized Georgia proclaiming, "Their talks breathed nothing but vengeance..." He wrote that the Creeks were a free nation and would not abide by any boundaries set by the Americans and British.[137]

Georgia officials urged Congress to allow the state, rather than the United States commissioners, to negotiate with the Creeks. They insisted on Georgians being present and were offended by being left out. Georgia did agree to provide a guard of 100 men for protection at the meeting.[138]

The commissioners went to Galphinton, Georgia, but McGillivray did not show up. Rather only two chiefs went with what McGillivray said were a few warriors. Others claimed there were 60.[139] After waiting for two weeks for more Creeks to show up, the commissioners said there were too few to negotiate with and left. Then, Georgia delegates took over the talks and declared that the U.S. commissioners were in violation of the state's rights. The next day the Georgians signed a treaty with the two chiefs confirming the controversial 1783 Augusta treaty and giving Georgia land east of the Oconee and Ockmulgee to the St. Mary's river. The enormous region that the two chiefs were giving away amounted to half of what would become present-day Georgia.[140]

McGillivray was outraged and denounced the Galphinton agreement. He said fewer than 20 Indians went to the negotiation and the few that did go went from motives of curiosity and were not of any consequence except the Tame King, who was well known to be but a roving beggar, going wherever he thought he could get gifts. McGillivray went on to say in a letter to Pensacola Governor O'Neill that the Americans blamed him for failure to resolve matters and attempted to bribe or assassinate him.[141] But the failure at Galphinton, he said, was because the commissioners did not notify the Creeks when and where to meet.[142]

McGillivray felt that he had to muster support from the rest of the Creek Nation. He issued orders to all the chiefs of the nation to attend an assembly to decide what action to take against the Americans settling on Creek hunting grounds. The Creek chiefs agreed to send resolutions to Georgia demanding that the colonists withdraw from land along the Oconee or face war.[143]

McGillivray and the chiefs feared that Georgians would persist in destroying the Creek Nation. McGillivray adamantly wrote in March 1786, letters to O'Neill that he and his people would not be merely spectators to destruction but had decided in their last general meeting to take arms in their defense and repel the invaders of their lands, to drive them from their encroachments and confine them to within their proper limits.

The Creek Nation had acted with moderation, he added. They had not immediately taken up arms upon learning that the Georgians were encroaching on their lands but optimistically submitted a petition to avert a crisis. McGillivray also needed assurance that Spain would back him. He asked O'Neill to notify the Georgians that they must leave the Creek lands free and that the region was under the protection of Spain.[144]

McGillivray warned that he would not give up land toward the Mississippi where Americans were settling.[145] War was at hand. There was no alternative since the Georgians had failed to enter into peace talks. Following the custom, sticks were sent to each town, one to be broken each day until April 23 as the day to set off for war. The Creeks were emboldened by their belief that the Spanish would help protect their lands. In fact, McGillivray was successful in getting the Spanish governors of Pensacola and New Orleans to agree to supply arms.

They were well aware of the fact that when Spain was settling the boundaries of its land with that of America in 1785, McGillivray wrote a proclamation for the chiefs of the Creek, Chickasaw and Cherokee Nations that the Indians would not abide by those set by the British and American Congress drawn from the treaty that ended the Revolutionary War.[146]

He urged his warriors to destroy colony settlements but to refrain from shedding blood unless it was in self-defense.[147] The Creeks drove settlers out, but the colonists returned the next winter. So, the confrontations continued.[148]

At this critical time, McGillivray was wracked by illness – gout, rheumatism and possibly venereal disease. He also might have been an alcoholic. But, despite his illness, he was determined to save the Creek Nation. He wrote to Miro that the Americans were "using every means in their power" to lure Creeks into agreements and trade, importing and exporting directly to and from London without heavy duties and charges. McGillivray said the Creek Nation was satisfied with goods from Panton but needed more and asked that duties be waived.[149]

The American superintendent for Indian affairs of the Southern District, James White, traveled to Creek country in 1787 to try to avoid the ever-threatening war. He was optimistic that if each side would give a little, Georgia and the Creeks could achieve peace.[150] McGillivray did receive White, preferring to deal with a United States official rather than Georgians, and the two corresponded a number of times.[151]

Georgia invited McGillivray to a conference at Shoulderbone Creek on October 15, 1786. McGillivray wrote back that he would never agree to give up the lands in question. He said he was too ill to travel until the following spring.

However, Fat King and Tame King, the two wayward chiefs, did attend the conference. The Lower Creek chiefs told the Georgians they were opposed to McGillivray. They rejected Georgia commissioners' wish to kill him. Still they were adamant in turning against McGillivray and declared to Georgians at the Treaty at Shoulderbone Creek that he was the principal person against them.

"He is from a large family, for which reason we will give him free passage to leave in peace," a Lower Creek chief said. "But we must get rid of him. If he wishes to live with the Spanish, he can go to them, or else he must die. It is not our desire to trick you, as up to now he has done. The talks and letters that McGillivray has sent you as the voice of the nation are not. They are of his own fabrication to serve his private ends and to make our nation poor."[152]

The Georgians took them hostage to force the Creek Nation to agree to the treaty terms. McGillivray ignored their demands. Tame King talked the Georgians into freeing him and the other chief, but five warriors were still held captive. American commissioner White met with McGillivray and other chiefs.

"Our lands are our life and breath," proclaimed Hollowing King, "if we part with them we part with our blood. We must fight for them."[153] White became convinced that the disputed land was vital to the Creeks and obtained the release of the five hostages.

Yet McGillivray's influence continued. One traveler, George Whitefield, praised the Creek chief, writing "his deportment was manly and collected."

Letters written by Spanish officials indicated McGillivray's power. He ruled with absolute authority "and whether he does it for love of the Sovereign, or for his private interests, it is necessary to favor a person, who uses his powerful influence with which he rules the Indians to the greatest advantage in the present circumstance," wrote Miro.

McGillivray "had the understanding of a white man and the cruel passions of an Indian," wrote Mobile commandant Vicente Folch.[154] McGillivray would not hesitate to kill for the sake of his beloved nation or in return of violence committed against those he knew. Several royalists stayed with him and obtained passports from him to make their way to Louisiana. On their way, led by McGillivray's servant, some of the men were killed by three murderers. McGillivray sent Milfort and warriors to hunt down the criminals. Two escaped but a third was hanged at what came to be called Murder Creek.[155]

McGillivray also could be sympathetic and kind. He gave a slave refuge and refused to give him up when the owner sent two Spaniards to get him. McGillivray threatened to use a razor to anyone who tried to capture the slave.[156] His humane side was evident when another tribe of Indians attacked a white family and McGillivray purchased the freedom of survivors who had been captured. He took them to a white settlement.[157]

The Spanish believed they had to continue to befriend McGillivray but did not entirely trust him. And to the colonists he was a force to be reckoned with.

Tensions escalated. McGillivray initiated attacks on Georgia settlements, including burning the town of Greensboro. Georgia Governor George Mathews rallied 3,000 troops to fight.[158] Georgia asked for a conference and McGillivray agreed but new governor George Handley postponed the meeting citing money problems.[159]

Meanwhile, the British courted McGillivray through William Augustus Bowles, who offered arms. Bowles traveled to Creek country and met with McGillivray. He said weapons were waiting for the Creeks in Florida, sent by English sympathizers. McGillivray then wrote to Miro and resigned his position as a Spanish agent. Miro asked him to reconsider. With this assurance, McGillivray turned his back on Bowles and, at Panton's advice, sent him away and said he would have no more dealings with him.[160] That, however, would not be the last of Bowles.

CHAPTER 4

SEEKING FEDERAL
INDIAN POLICY

When George Washington was unanimously elected the new nation's first president in 1789, he faced the immediate crisis of the war between Georgia and the Creeks. As a British officer he had had experience with Indian affairs long before becoming a Revolutionary War hero. In fact, a mission that involved Indians made him a much-admired officer when he was only 21 years old and helped shape his view toward Indians.

Not unlike other major land owners, his father owned a Virginia estate of 10,000 acres that had been taken from Indians. Washington might have felt guilty when he heard first hand the plight of Indians while on his first significant military mission.

In 1753, Virginia Governor Robert Dinwiddie sent him to a wild frontier, called Ohio Country. Washington carried a letter from the British demanding that the French leave the region, setting the stage for the preamble to the French and Indian War. During that trip, Washington met Seneca Chief Tanacharison of the Iroquois, called Half-King. The chief would serve as a guide and representative of Indians in meeting with the French.[161]

The young Washington listened intently to Half-King tell the French that his people had lived on the land for 300 years. The chief's impassioned plea to the French convinced Washington that Indians must be treated fairly. "If you had come in a peaceable Manner like our Brethren the English, we should not have been against your trading with us as they do, but to come, Fathers, & build great houses upon our Land, & to take it by Force, is what we cannot submit to," Half-King told the French. He noted that the French and the English were both white. The Indians live in a land that does not belong either to one or the other, he said, but that the "GREAT BEING" above allowed it to be the home of Indians.[162]

Washington admiringly quoted the chief's words and devoted many passages to the Indian in a journal detailing his expedition. His notes were widely published in American newspapers and British magazines. Though the French refused to leave, Washington's vivid description of the wilderness and his trek through knee-deep snow and across icy rivers caught the attention of the colonists.

Yet, in another experience Washington battled Indians. In 1775, he served under British General Edward Braddock who was opposing the French. Braddock had made the mistake of alienating the Indians who joined forces with the French. He also failed to listen to Washington's advice to send fewer than the general's 2,000 troops through Indian country to capture the French fort. The mission was a disaster. Washington barely escaped death, with two of his mounts shot as he rode them. Nearly 1,000 men were killed. Braddock was wounded.

Washington led a retreat that was hailed as valiant. Braddock died a few days later. Washington buried him and ran wagons over the grave to camouflage it so the Indians would not dig up the body and scalp the general.[163]

He then was named commander of the British Virginia Regiment, which had just been formed with more than 1,000 men. His job was to protect the huge region from Indians, a task he said was impossible.[164]

So, the new nation's first president came into office with two conflicting views of the issue between Indians and settlers. His trusted advisor Henry Knox would prod him to an honorable path in deciding what to do about the conflict between newly arrived colonists and long time Indian dwellers.

The new nation's policy would come down to a matter of trust and admiration between Washington and Knox. They had formed a strong relationship during the Revolutionary War when Knox had served as Washington's special lieutenant over eight years of war.[165] He was Washington's artillery commander and would be of vital importance in a significant victory in the war.[166]

Their backgrounds were entirely different. Oddly enough, Knox, as Washington's conscience on Indian affairs, lacked experience with Indians. But he was a man of high morals and a deep conviction that America should be shaped by its path toward justice. He believed fervently that since the patriots fought for their own freedom, it would be disgraceful to oppose the Indians who only wanted recognition of their just claims.

He had known hardship even as a child. Knox's father deserted the family in Boston when his shipbuilding business went broke and young Henry, not even 12, had to quit a prestigious private school to help support his mother and younger brother by working in a bookstore. He continued his education himself; he was particularly fond of reading the classics, talking at length with military veterans about their adventures and reading volumes of military science.[167]

Known as one of the best fighters in a street gang, he went on to join the local regiment called The Train. As a volunteer, and by reading scores of military books, Knox learned all about cannons – how to load, fire and maintain them. In just a few years, this knowledge would make him a young hero like Washington.[168]

In a hunting accident, he accidentally shot off two fingers and from then on kept his hand wrapped in a handkerchief or scarf. He bought his own bookstore and married. His best friend was Nathanael Greene and they spent hours talking about military strategy. Another friendly visitor to his bookstore was Paul Revere. When the war began and the British took Boston, Knox and his wife, Lucy, escaped by boat in the middle of the night.[169]

Knox made his way to a colonial camp in Cambridge where he heard that patriots had captured Fort Ticonderoga in upstate New York with its bounty of 78 cannons and other munitions.[170] The fact that Ticonderoga was almost 300 miles away did not deter Knox.

He convinced the new commander, General George Washington, to have Congress authorize him to retrieve the cannons. Washington agreed, having admired Knox's military experience in weapons. Knox assured him that he could bring the cannons back to Massachusetts. [171]

Knox wrote to Washington telling him of the challenge before him. Even getting the cannons and mortars from the fort to the landing would be difficult he said. And the passage across the lake would be even more precarious and could take 10 days.

The journey began with a bitter winter wind and heavy snowstorm. Then, at Ticonderoga he would have to cross a lake with 11-foot cannons weighed 5,000 pounds each. How to get them over that water was daunting. There were 59 cannons and mortars weighing 60 tons.[172]

With the raw power of oxen and horses, he pulled the artillery to the lake. Then the men had to maneuver various boats and barges to try to get the munitions over before ice, which was already forming, froze the surface. One vessel sunk but they were able to rescue it.

Timing would be critical. If the ice and snow held, sledding would enable the men to transport the cannons, but if not, the roads would be gullied and make it impossible to move.[173]

Knox prayed for snow and arranged for 42 sleds and 160 oxen to haul the cannon and mortars to Springfield, Massachusetts. A thaw slowed the mission but on Christmas Day two feet of snow fell and the soldiers were able to move on, cheered along the way by the locals. The journey took 56 stressful days.[174]

Now, they desperately needed gun powder. Pleas to all the colonies finally resulted in Connecticut sending 3,000 pounds. Knox's completion of the monumental task would turn the tide of the war. The patriots successfully drove the British from Boston with Knox's Ticonderoga cannons. Historians have called the victory one of the most important in America because it signaled to the colonists that they could win their fight for freedom against the British.[175]

After the war was won in 1783, the new nation laid claim to all of the country east of the Mississippi except for lands of the Indians. Who would rule that vast frontier? The Articles of Confederation left the matter ambivalent. The central government under the Articles was regarded as a coordinating body without power to control the nation as a whole. Many colonists wanted states to go their separate ways.[176] The Articles did somewhat address the Indian issue, saying that states had the authority to regulate trade with Indians.

Washington and Knox, however, advocated a central government for the new nation. Washington lamented that the country was failing to become unified. He believed that a central government was essential, but that idea was highly controversial.[177] Washington wanted to step out of public life, but he agreed after much reluctance to be a delegate to a convention to replace the Articles of Confederation with a more empowered national government.[178]

The Constitutional Convention began meeting in Philadelphia on May 29, 1787, after a number of postponements for lack of a quorum.[179] Over the next few months, delegates finally approved a new central government but without providing for a federal veto over state legislation.[180] After nearly a year of intense debate, the Constitution was finally ratified by the states.[181]

American commissioners, appointed to deal with Indians, kept McGillivray apprised of the new government. He found himself the leader of a region in a country that was still evolving. McGillivray wrote to Miro on September 20, 1788, that plans for negotiating a treaty were postponed until spring in part because a new government was being formed and that the new Congress would be sending instructions. However, Georgians were not abiding by a truce. "Thus we find that the Georgians will Counteract the Intentions of Congress," he wrote.[182]

Washington hoped the U.S. commissioners could make peace and put an end to the Creek relationship with Spain.[183]

Several months later, when another treaty invitation came from the commissioners, McGillivray was in the Lower Creek towns meeting with chiefs who had already sent warriors to fight Georgians. He had been told that the commissioners had been instructed to abide by the wishes of Georgians, but he was encouraged that the whole matter was being referred to Washington "who is vested with nearly royal Powers" for his judgment that would be adopted by Congress. McGillivray would not abide by the Georgian effort to seize lands and control Creek trade. He asked Spanish governor of New Orleans Miro to supply more ammunition and arms.[184]

While the nation's new leaders grappled with how to govern their country, McGillivray not only faced the new American government but was also in a precarious position with Spain. Miro told Folch, Spanish governor of Mobile, to stop correspondence with McGillivray so that all contact would be through him. He had tried to persuade McGillivray to make peace with the Americans because a full-scale war would erode Spanish control. So, he reduced arms to the Creeks.

McGillivray met with his adversary Bowles, who was still trying to get the Creek trade. Bowles, described as a scoundrel by McGillivray allies, portrayed himself as an agent for England to supply goods and arms to the Creeks. He wanted to get the business that had been going to Panton, Leslie in Pensacola.[185] But Bowles was unable to deliver many supplies and McGillivray turned against him.[186] Bowles would become a serious threat.

Meanwhile, commissioners tried to reassure McGillivray that Washington had good intentions. "We are now governed by a president who is like the old King over the great water," they wrote. "He Commands all the Warriors of the thirteen great fires."[187] They assured him that Washington would see that justice would prevail.[188]

To his credit in striving for justice, Washington made Knox his Secretary of War. The post would become critical in dealing with Indian affairs. Knox reported that the Continental Congress had harmed the Indians by grabbing territory east of the Mississippi River. Knox hated the idea that they were being driven from their homelands. Some tribes were becoming extinct, he wrote to Washington. "If the same causes continue," he said, "the same effects will happen and in a short period the idea of an Indian on this side of the Mississippi will only be found in the page of the historian."[189]

Knox succeeded in getting Washington to make Indian policy his top priority. "The government of the United States are determined that their Administration of Indian Affairs shall be directed entirely by the great principles of Justice and humanity," Washington emphasized in a letter to the commissioners attempting to negotiate a treaty with the southern Indians.[190]

The president well knew that Knox was right and that the future of relations with Indians was at a critical stage in the north and south of America. Both regions were on the verge of war.[191]

Even though Indian territory covered the eastern third of North America, the tribes had been given no say in the treaty with Great Britain. One proposal was to gradually edge them west.[192] Some colonists even urged Washington to declare war against Indians. But the Creeks alone had 6,000 warriors compared to only 600 United States soldiers.[193]

Knox adamantly opposed going to war and continued to believe that the new government must adhere to the conscience of the American Revolution."[194] Knox firmly maintained that the government must respect the rights of Indians to their land.[195] "In other words, the very principles of the American Revolution claimed to stand for were at stake," noted historian Joseph J. Ellis in "The McGillivray Moment."[196]

Knox believed that state treaties with Indians had been violated. States and settlers broke promises. He had read pleas from tribes begging that their territory be respected. And by Washington's side during the eight-year travails of the Revolutionary War he absorbed the liberties they were fighting for and insisted that the new nation should uphold those principles.[197]

Knox was delighted when, in the summer of 1789, Washington asked him to assess the Indian tribes between the Alleghenies and the Mississippi. Washington viewed that region as America's future since it would be settled by white men already pouring into the Ohio Valley. Yet he agreed with Knox that Indians should be dealt with fairly and that justice should prevail. The dilemma was to protect Indian rights while allowing whites to settle on the newly won land.[198]

Tribes should be considered as foreign nations, not as the subjects of any particular state, Knox advised. That approach meant that only the U.S. government, rather than the states, would have the right to make treaties and essentially would give control to Washington, Secretary of State Thomas Jefferson and himself as Secretary of War.[199]

However, the matter was confusing because Congress had passed the ordinance in 1786 giving itself the authority to regulate trade and manage Indian affairs but without infringing or violating states rights. Then, the new Constitution gave Congress the authority to regulate foreign and Indian trade despite several states, including Georgia, already negotiating treaties on their own. Knox interpreted the Constitution to mean that control rested with the executive branch.

In response to Washington's request, Knox reviewed treaties states had made and their results and wrote a series of letters to Washington expressing his thoughts on the Indian issue. Knox noted that the Creek Nation consisted of upper and lower districts of about 100 towns and that McGillivray carried much influence.

The State of Georgia was engaged in a serious war with the Creeks, Knox wrote to Washington. The United States should consider becoming involved in the dispute and examine the issues, he said.

He outlined the three treaties between Georgia and the Creeks and said the Indians did not recognize them because only the chiefs of two towns agreed to the land cessations.[200]

To Knox's credit, he advised that a nation built on the basis of justice should refrain from injury to any of its people. If the Indians derive their subsistence chiefly by hunting, and must encroach on the land of another tribe they might destroy each other, he warned.

"The Indians being the prior occupants possess the right of the Soil," he wrote. "It cannot be taken from them unless by their free consent, or by the right of Conquest in case of a just War —

To dispossess them on any other principle would be a gross violation of the fundamental Laws of Nature and of that distributive justice which is the glory of a nation."[201]

Knox estimated that there were about 76,000 Indians east of the Mississippi and north of the Ohio. A conciliatory approach to incorporating them into the United States for 50 years would cost about $15,000 a year, he wrote. Coercion and oppression would cost much more, he said. "But the blood and injustice which would stain the character of the nation, would be beyond all pecuniary calculation," he continued.[202]

After reading the three treaties of Georgia with the Creeks, Knox reported their contents to Washington in a letter dated July 6, 1789, and explained that war had ensued because McGillivray had refused to acknowledge them since only two chiefs had agreed to the terms. Congress had warned the Creeks that if they failed to obey treaty promises, the arms of the United States would be used to protect the frontier.[203]

The next day, Knox wrote another letter to Washington telling him that if the United States decided to wage war, other Indian nations would likely join the Creeks.[204] Also, the region of Spain would have to be considered, he said. Spain actually claimed much of that territory ceded by Great Britain to the United States.

Congress had two alternatives. The first would be to use arms to force the Creeks to agree to a treaty and to protect Georgia. The second would be to appoint three special commissioners to go to Georgia and conclude a peace with the Creeks and other tribes south of the Ohio..[205]

Some 5,000 warriors would probably be the size of an Indian army, Knox estimated. The war would probably last for two years and cost $1.5 million a year. "A less army than the one herein proposed would probably be utterly inadequate to the object: an useless expence, and disgraceful to the nation," he added.

A far better alternative, Knox advised, would be the appointment of the three commissioners who would be paid to negotiate a treaty. They would have the power to resolve boundary disputes between the Creeks and Georgia without being restrained by previous treaties. To enforce the treaty, 500 troops would be assigned to the territory.

A court martial would try those who failed to abide by the treaties, he said. That would convince the Indians that the honorable and good intentions of the United States would provide security against the injustice of lawless frontier people.[206]

Knox recommended that a law should be passed declaring that Indian tribes would possess the right of all lands in their territory. They would only give up territory agreed to in bona fide purchases made under the authority of the United States. Indians would be considered as foreign nations, not as the subjects of any particular state. Colonists could not be prevented from settling on the territory but would be restrained and regulated, he explained, so that they would not intrude on Indian lands. Since game would be diminished, Indians would be given sheep, cattle and gifts as well as help by missionaries in cultivating their lands.[207] The Creek economy was already shifting from hunting to agriculture.[208]

The new Constitution required Washington to obtain the advice and consent of the Senate. So, he and Knox went to the Senate on August 22, 1789, to present their case for fair treatment of Indians. Washington asked Senators to appoint the three commissioners who would negotiate a fair treaty that would be enforced.

To conciliate the powerful tribes of southern Indians, amounting probably to 14,000 warriors, and "to attach them firmly to the United States," should be a major goal of government," he said. That effort would not only bring peace and security to the whole southern frontier, but would form a barrier against any European power that might one day become an enemy of the United States.

"The fate of the southern States therefore, or the neighboring Colonies, may principally depend on the present measures of the Union towards the southern Indians," Washington stressed.

He noted that the commissioners should reassure the Cherokees, Choctaws and Chickasaws of good intentions and friendship of the United States and that trade would be forthcoming.

"But the case of the Creek Nation is of the highest importance and requires an immediate decision," he continued. He attributed hostilities between Georgia and the Creeks to disagreement concerning the three treaties made at Augusta in 1783, at Galphinton in 1785, and at Shoulderbone in 1786. Georgia asserts that the treaties should be abided by while the Creeks deny the validity of them, he noted.

The commissioners should evaluate the treaties with impartiality, Washington said, adding that Georgia should be represented. It would be embarrassing for Georgia to have to give up the land that had been conveyed by the previous treaties and settled. So the commissioners should strive to negotiate with the Creeks a conveyance of the disputed lands, Washington advised. To that effect, he stressed that the commissioners should determine if the treaties were fair and representative of the Creek Nation.[209]

Senators were hesitant. They demanded to see all the Georgia treaties and possibly refer the matter to a committee. "This defeats every purpose of my coming here," Washington retorted. The Senate decided to postpone the matter until

Monday. The president agreed, motioned to Knox and strode out with a discontented air.

Two days later Washington, described as more serene, had presented the Senate with a written document beforehand.[210] This time the Senate approved three commissioners who would negotiate a treaty that would override previous ones. The commissioners were Benjamin Lincoln, a general in the Continental Army, Cyrus Griffin, last president of the Continental Congress, and David Humphreys, an aide to Washington.[211]

If the commissioners judged that the three treaties were valid and obtained with free consent and if the Creeks refused, the Union would use arms to enforce the provisions in them. But if the commissioners found the treaties not represented by the Creek Nation or unfair, compensation would be paid to the Creeks and a line of Union military posts would protect their remaining territory.[212]

Even as the new government in New York was trying to address the country's number one issue of Indian policy, a new development in Georgia would escalate the threat to the Creek Nation.

CHAPTER 5

GEORGIA POWDER KEG

As Knox and Washington struggled to create a fair and just Indian policy, land companies were poised to take even more Creek territory. Speculators were offered prime parcels by three Yazoo companies, the Virginia Yazoo Company, the South Carolina Yazoo Company and the Tennessee Company. In 1790, they bought more than 24 million acres from the Georgia legislature for $200,000. That enormous territory extended over much of what is now Alabama, Mississippi and Tennessee.[213] Yazoo tried to bribe McGillivray with shares in the company so that he would not be a threat to the influx of settlers that would come onto the lands. McGillivray refused and later learned that several Georgia legislators had plotted to have him killed.[214]

With an escalating war between Georgia and the Creeks imminent, Knox believed that white settlers taking over Indian land would destroy the Indians to a greater extent than Spanish explorers wiped out the Aztecs.[215]

McGillivray ambitiously risked high stakes negotiations with the Spanish that if successful could protect his land or if not lead to its demise. He did not want to meet the United States commissioners, but Miro, the Spanish official, urged him in a letter to go and force the Americans' hand. Spain was afraid that a full-scale war between the United States and the Creeks would erode Spanish power in the region. Miro said McGillivray's attendance at the meeting would promote the tranquility of the Creek Nation "and in any event the world would know the reasonableness of your part, if it is necessary to continue the war, if you renewed the conferences, showing in them that the Creeks are a free nation that can not be obliged to cede the lands that the Georgians have usurped…," Miro wrote. Should the Americans refuse to agree to a just treaty, Spain would be in a better position to protect the Creeks, he added.[216]

McGillivray asked the commissioners to delay the meeting for a few weeks until mid-September and they agreed. He wrote to Miro that he would consider himself fortunate if he could induce them to conclude a peace on satisfactory terms that would assure the Creek Nation the peaceful enjoyment of its rights. The Americans brought about the Revolutionary War, he said, with high ideals of gaining independence by conquering the New World.

"It is well & generally known that the War in which we have so long been engaged in with the Americans was of their own Seeking," he claimed. In the dream of greatness and power, he said, they thought that they could seize with impunity every foot of territory belonging to the "Red Natives" of America and that it would be easy to exterminate them if necessary.[217]

McGillivray wrote to Panton just before the negotiations that a major part of any treaty would hinge on trade and that he would not break off the existing arrangement with Spain. However, he then stressed that Spain would have to guarantee more support and not have a repeat of the previous summer when they had reduced supplies to the Creeks. He complained that the Spanish guns were inferior to those previously gotten from the British. He essentially warned that if the Spanish treated the Creeks shabbily, he would take the Indian trade to the Americans.

Miro had suggested to McGillivray that he persuade the Americans to settle west of the Mississippi and McGillivray said that would allow peace, that his warriors would not follow them there. But during this period, McGillivray was aware of more threats to assassinate him, noting that someone had been murdered in the house of his sister.[218]

Then, McGillivray became offended that the Spanish payments to him were not substantial enough. The "pittance" that was given to him was a disgrace, unworthy of his position, he wrote to Panton. If Spain wanted his services, they should establish a regular salary as England had done, providing two interpreters, one among the Upper and one among the Lower Towns. If payment was not sufficient, he would have to get funds from his American estate to maintain the interpreters and himself. He asked what he should do.

He had no reason to hope that disputes with Americans would be resolved but he planned to go to the meeting to refute any suggestion that he was unjust and unreasonable. And he wanted the Americans to return to him the property of his father.[219]

McGillivray set off for the meeting at Rock Landing on the Oconee River in central Georgia. He took with him an impressive force of warriors — some say 900[220] while others put the figure at 2,000.[221] McGillivray himself said in a letter to Panton that he took with him 900 chosen men and that the U.S. commissioners had with them about 400 men in arms.[222]

The commissioners arrived on September 20, 1789, and were welcomed by McGillivray who reportedly seemed to want peace. Creek warriors camped on the western bank of the river and the commissioners set up camp on the eastern bank. The first two days the commissioners and McGillivray talked privately, with McGillivray being polite and courteous. Then the commissioners crossed the river and participated in a black drink ceremony with the chiefs.

"The next day McGillivray dined with us, & although he got very much intoxicated, he seemed to retain his recollection & reason, beyond what I had ever seen in a person, when in the same condition," Humphreys later wrote to Washington. "At this time, I became intimate to a certain degree with him & endeavored to extract his real sentiments & feelings, in a conversation alone, confidentially. He declared he was really desirous of a peace, that the local situation of the Creeks required that they should be connected with us rather than with any other People, that, however they had certain advantages in the Treat with Spain, in respect to a guarantee & Trade, which they ought not in justice to themselves to give up without an equivalent."

But the event was probably doomed from the start. The key players, Humphreys and McGillivray, lacked respect for each other. Humphreys complained to Washington that McGillivray's countenance lacked openness and his Indian attire was slovenly. "In short, he appears to have the good sense of an American, the shrewdness of a Scotchman, & the cunning of an Indian," Humphreys wrote. "I think he is so much addicted to debauchery that he will not live four years." He added that McGillivray's influence was probably as great as they had believed and his services might be very important if he would sincerely accept the interests of the United States.[223]

McGillivray wrote "that puppy Humphries" threatened to cram down Creek throats objectionable articles in a proposed treaty.[224] One article stipulated that the Creeks would be under the protection of the United States only. That would present a problem with the Indian relationship with Spain and usurp Creek independence. And the proposal would require McGillivray to give up the Oconee Lands, leaving the boundary made at Augusta, Shoulderbone and Galphinton. The Americans would guarantee to the Creeks land west of that line. Free trade would be established at numerous ports with the Indians getting the same terms as U.S. citizens. All prisoners and goods taken would be returned.[225]

Humphreys was very dissatisfied with McGillivray, calling him frivolous and unjustifiable in nature. He was dismayed that McGillivray objected to previous treaties that were not binding because he had not approved them and that any agreement with Georgia had to be fully agreed to by the Creek Nation. An Indian trader said McGillivray was concerned that he would have to break relations with the Spanish to treat with the American government. Humphreys said that was not the case but that if McGillivray could not be compatible with both he should decide which to be tied to. He offended McGillivray by saying that he didn't speak for the entire Creek Nation.[226]

The commissioners read the proposed treaty. McGillivray and the chiefs met privately. Humphreys claimed that the chiefs indicated their sincere desire for peace, some even shedding tears, but the chiefs said that they could not declare peace without McGillivray, who was sick.

The next morning McGillivray sent a letter to the commissioners refusing to agree to the treaty and informing them that he and his entourage were leaving. He did say he would meet with the Americans again in the future and would agree to a truce during the winter.

The commissioners had been instructed to offer the Creeks payment for the disputed land but apparently did not. McGillivray retreated and sent a message to the commissioners that he left to feed his horses and that he was ill. But he also said that he was returning home because Creek land was not returned in the treaty, deferring the matter until the next spring. "We sincerely desire a peace, but cannot sacrifice much to obtain it," he wrote. He concluded by saying that Congress had declared the U.S. would be just and humane in dealing with the Indians and he expected that stance to prevail.[227]

McGillivray was ill and disheartened when he returned home. He wrote to Panton, "I arrived three days ago from the Oconee, sick, disgusted & fatigued to death."[228]

The arts of flattery, ambition and intimidation were exhausted in vain, McGillivray wrote to Panton. "I at last told him by G__ I would not have such a Treaty cram'd down my throat," he said. Upon departing, he had told his warriors that it had been unlikely that the Americans would do the Creeks justice. "…my opinion was that we came in a body," he wrote, "so we should retreat as peaceably as we came, and not to be laying there wrangling with them, lest bad consequences might ensue."[229] Yet, the Creeks wanted to appear to be in favor of avoiding war and sent Washington a fan of white eagle tails as a peace symbol.[230]

Though the Rock Landing negotiations ended without an agreement, the matter was far from over. And McGillivray was not unhappy with all United States officials. He had come to admire some of the Americans, particularly General Andrew Pickens, who had met with him on several occasions. "Pickens I take to be a worthy moderate man: We got well acquainted, and I am sure if he had remained in his appointment, we should have come to some agreement," McGillivray wrote.[231]

Always the diplomat, McGillivray hoped that his allies would approve of his conduct in negotiations as he was determined to be honest and not sacrifice the interests of Creek friends and their own political good faith to private interest and mercenary motive. He noted that he did not accept presents Washington had sent and forbade his warriors to accept gifts.

On the other hand, Humphreys concluded that the failure to reach peace was the fault of McGillivray alone. "It is a melancholy consideration to reflect that a whole Nation must sometimes perish for the sins of one man," he wrote in his report.[232]

An article in the *Salem Mercury* in Massachusetts proclaimed that McGillivray refused to agree to a treaty but that all the other chiefs appeared extremely desirous of being at peace with the United States.[233] At least one historian speculated that Panton caused the failure of Rock Landing.[234]

The stage was set for a major confrontation. Commissioners from Rock Landing recommended that the United States invade Creek country. Indian agent Benjamin Hawkins, however, warned that American planners of Indian policy would have a lot of explaining to do when they reached the pearly gates and had to defend the treatment of the native people. One chief angrily proclaimed, "We are made by the same hand and in the same shape with yourselves."[235]

Washington reported to the Senate that the commissioners attributed the failure of the treaty to McGillivray. But McGillivray blamed the failure on the influence of Georgia. Washington outlined details of a military plan if a treaty could not be successfully negotiated. Six forts would be built to protect Georgians, and if necessary five regiments of 700 men each would be deployed. Washington estimated that the Creeks had some 4,500 warriors from about 80 towns.[236]

However, the president was not ready to give up on peace talks. He and Knox came up with another plan.

CHAPTER 6

Washington
Aims for Justice

Georgia congressmen urged the president to declare war against the Creeks. But George Washington was a man of mission and refused to give up on crafting an Indian policy that would be honorable. Others in his administration, including Indian agents, Thomas Jefferson and Henry Knox, shared his admirable view and the new president must have been buoyed by the support of those trusted advisors.

Benjamin Hawkins, American representative to the Creeks and a North Carolina senator, wrote to Thomas Jefferson who was in Paris to bring him up to date on the issue.

"You will see by the Treaties which I enclose how attentive I have been to the rights of these people; and I can assure you there is nothing I have more at heart than the preservation of them," Hawkins wrote. The Creeks were in danger of losing everything but their name, he lamented.

Action by Congress without the cooperation of the southern states would be ineffectual and Georgia and North Carolina refused to recognize the right of the federal government to regulate Indian affairs. Hawkins put the issue in moral terms, implying that destroying the native populations would amount to a sin that would require an "account" before higher authority. But he had no solution to the dilemma posed by federalism; what recourse would the federal government have when states deny its authority? Hawkins and Knox articulated the view that the

Indians had the right to the land and that, for the states to share it, boundaries must be set between the territories of the American settlers and Indians. This was in direct conflict with the position of the states, which claimed lands virtually without limit, treating the Creeks as mere "tenants at will" who must leave the land if the states required it. The only power the states conceded to the federal government was the right to generally regulate trade.

Jefferson commended Hawkins for taking a moral position on the rights of Indians and said that to believe otherwise would be a source of dishonor to the American character. The two principles on which the United States should conduct policy towards the Indians are justice and fear, he believed.

"After the injuries we have done them they cannot love us," Jefferson wrote, "which leaves us no alternative but that of fear to keep them from attacking us, but justice is what we should never lose sight of & in time it may recover their esteem."[237]

So, the new government of the United States was critically divided, with the Indian issue at stake. A solution would not be easy.

Knox stood by his beliefs and continued to urge the president to avoid war. On February 15, 1790, he wrote an impassioned analysis for Washington. "The serious crisis of affairs, in which the United States are involved with the Creeks requires that every honorable and probable expedient that can be devised should be used to avert a War with that tribe..." Knox said.

As Secretary of War, he warned Washington that young Creek warriors were on the brink of ignoring chiefs who tried to keep the peace. Coupled with lawless colonists, hostilities were on the horizon. Fighting with the Creeks, he added, could lead to complications since the Lower Creeks lived in Spanish territory and the Creek Nation was on friendly terms with Spain. The connection of the Creeks to the colonies of west and east Florida must be considered, Knox said.

"In case of a War with the Creeks," he wrote, "and they should be pushed to take refuge within the limits of either of the aforesaid Colonies, the United States would be reduced to a most embarrassed predicament – For they must either follow the Creeks in order to extinguish the War; establish posts in their country; or retire: In the first case, they would seriously be embroiled with Spain – In the second, the operation would be extremely hazardous and expensive – In the third the impression made would not be attended with adequate or permanent effects to the expence incurred by the expedition."[238]

The Indian commissioners had proposed to send the draft of a treaty for the Creeks to sign, but that measure could lead to war, Knox advised. "For if such treaty should be transmitted to the Creeks, with a declaration that they must receive and sign it, or War should ensue, it is highly probable that the latter event would take place by an irruption of the Creeks, long before the Messenger could reach the seat of Government," he wrote.

Knox told the president that in search of ways to avert the evils impending on the Indian question he had had repeated conversations with Hawkins, who was honorable and well acquainted with the Creeks. Knox noted that Hawkins felt pretty strongly that at this time McGillivray was opposed to a war with the United States and that Hawkins believed the influential chief would gladly embrace any rational means that would be offered to achieve peace.

Knox reported that Hawkins believed McGillivray might be willing to travel to the seat of government in New York to negotiate if security would be provided. Knox went on to stress that the overture was certainly worth trying. He had sent Hawkins the draft of a letter to McGillivray. Hawkins agreed with what the letter said and would add comments of his own.

The bearer of the letter ought to be a man of real talents and judgment, Knox noted. Although the ostensible object should be to deliver the letter, the main mission should be much more extensive, he said. "He should be capable of observing the effects of the proposition, on the mind of Mr McGillivray and the other chiefs – He should be of such character and manners as to insinuate himself into their confidence – of obviating their objections to the proposition – of exhibiting in still stronger colours than the letter the ruinous effects of a War to the Creeks — In the prosecution of his designs he should not be in a hurry – but wait with attention and patience the symptoms of compliance – confirm them in such dispositions – and be calm and firm when opposed – And if after all his labor and exertions he should fail of success, he should be capable of giving a clear narrative of the means he used, and the obstacles which prevented his success," Knox wrote.

"On this persons negociation, would depend much blood and treasure and in any event the reputation of the United States," he observed.

Then he gave Washington a rundown of the cost. The trip would probably take four months and if compensation was $8 a day would amount to $960, plus expenses of $400. It would cost at least $1,000 more to bring chiefs to New York, plus gifts to them and the cost of their return trip to Creek country.

"But there cannot be any doubt of the economy of the proposed application of the money herein required when compared with the expence which must attend a War," Knox stressed.[239]

He then noted that the consequences could be successful and prevent a war or fail with the United States government having tried to reach peace. And he requested a passport for McGillivray from the time of the Creeks entering the United States until their return to their own country.[240]

Washington decided that negotiating face to face with McGillivray and Creek headsmen at the center of power with the highest officials of the United States government would be successful.

The president revealed his thoughts in his diary:

> Exercised on horseback between 9 and 11 o'clock. On my return had a long conversation with Colo. Willet, who was engaged to go as a private agent, but for public purposes, to Mr. McGillivray, principal Chief of the Creek Nation. In this conversation he was impressed with the critical situation of our affairs with that Nation — the importance of getting him and some other Chiefs to this City — with such lures as respected McGillivray personally, and might be held out to him. His Colo. Willet's going was not to have the appearance of a governmental act – he and the business he went upon, would be introduced to McGillivray by Colo. Hawkins, of the Senate from North Carolina who was a correspondent of McGillivray's – but he would be provided with a passport for him and other Indian Chiefs, if they inclined to make use of it; but not to part with it if they did not. The letter from Colo. Hawkins to McGillivray was calculated to bring to his and the view of the Creek Nation the direful consequences of a rupture with the United States. The disposition of the general government to deal justly and honorable by them – and the means by which they, the Creeks, may avert the calamities of war, which must be brought on by the disorderly people of both Nations, if a Senate, which had only to ratify the Treaty of New York before adjourning gave the President a free hand."[241]

So, Hawkins, who had corresponded successfully with McGillivray, was chosen to introduce Willett by letter. Willett, a native of Long Island, New York, had been a distinguished officer in the Revolutionary War.[242] Hawkins wrote in his introductory letter on March 6, 1790, urging McGillivray to travel to New York that he was surprised that the meeting at Rock Landing was a failure.

Hawkins wrote that he was sincere in his desire that the United States should be on friendly terms with the Southern Indians and that the relationship should be based on justice and humanity. He cautioned McGillivray that the failure to reach an agreement at Rock Landing put the Creeks in a very critical situation.

The United States cannot advance one step further, he wrote, having already proceeded to the utmost lengths that could be required by the principles of justice or humanity and would not be responsible for any consequences that might ensue, however dreadful.

Hawkins told McGillivray that he and the other chiefs seemed to want to preserve the peace but that the Indians could not prevent hostilities, therefore arose the extreme danger to which the Creek Nation was exposed. "If you strike," he said, "the U. States *must punish,* it will then become a Contest of power the events of which may be disagreeable and expensive to the United States, but the result must be ruin to the Creeks.

"To prevent the Calamities which will ensue to Your Nation from a war, well deserves your anxious Concern," Hawkins wrote. "Reflect well upon the Creeks & Compare their force with the power of the United States."

Hawkins told McGillivray that if he would travel to New York to put the Creek case before the president, "I will answer with my Honour & my life that you will be received & treated with, on the footing of Justice & humanity."

McGillivray and other Creek chiefs had been granted a passport for safe travels, Hawkins explained. Willett, the bearer of the letter is a gentleman of honor who has been told the contents of the letter and can be talked with freely, he said, adding that he was sure McGillivray will give him every attention that might be required.

"Remember that the United States are disposed to be favorable and friendly to you and that I Shall rejoice if my efforts Should prove Serviceable to your Nation," he concluded.[243]

Knox met with Willett and explained the crisis situation with the Creeks. Then Washington met with Willett. The president told him Georgia did not want a peace treaty but wanted Congress to provide a force to subdue the Creeks. That would require $15 million and considerable troops from northern states. Washington hoped Willett could invite the Creeks to New York to treat without Georgia knowing about it.[244]

The plan was to be totally secret, with only trusted General Andrew Pickens, who had served successfully as a commissioner to the Indians and was admired by McGillivray, to know of the mission and help along the way.

Washington's selection of Willett proved to be a wise choice. The United States was on the cusp of solving a crisis that the new country could not avoid and the choice of messenger to Creek country was critically important. If Willett could convince McGillivray to gather Creek chiefs for a trip to New York to negotiate in person with the powers of the country, there was a chance that there could be a peaceful resolution to the question of who ultimately had control of the vast lands that had been the Creeks' home for generations.

CHAPTER 7

MESSENGER OF HOPE

Willett left New York on March 15, 1790, on a sloop bound for Charleston, South Carolina with a servant and two horses. He kept a journal of his travel to the Creek Nation. The voyage to the Southern coastal town took 14 days. When his servant became fearful and retreated back to New York, a German helper took his place.[245]

A few days after landing at Charleston, Willett arrived at General Pickens' plantation on the Savannah River. Pickens gave him an Indian guide named Young Corn to accompany him through Cherokee country. Willett bought two more horses, one for the guide and the other for supplies.[246] On April 19, with the servant riding in a sulky loaded with baggage and Willett and Young Corn on horseback, the party headed into Indian country.[247]

The very next day Willett met with disaster. After spending the night at a colonel's house one of his horses took fright, ran away, overturned his load, and wounded his leg. "So that we got only twenty-four miles on our journey." He did not say what happened to the horse. "Encamped in the woods, at a branch of good water; got myself a neat hut built; supped on chocolate; and had a very comfortable lodging on my bear-skin and blanket."[248]

Willett left at sunrise the next morning and a few hours later arrived at a Cherokee town where he bought corn for his horses. He crossed the mountains in a hailstorm then rode for about 28 miles that day through mountainous country. He continued through towns that ranged in size from 16 to 50 houses. Along the way he stayed with a trader who Willett gave a letter of introduction.

The trader, Thomas Gogg, who had lived with the Cherokees, introduced Willett to Chief Yellow Bird. The chief invited Willett to an exciting ball game. Willett proceeded to the town of peace, Eustenaree near present day Calhoun, Georgia, where Cherokees shed no blood. Interestingly, he discovered that the town, on the banks of a river, was a haven for those guilty of crimes. He had an introductory letter to two chiefs, Badger and Jobberson, who were hospitable to him.[249] They told him the shortest and best route to the Creek Nation. Unfortunately, he had to back track a bit.

After a few more days traveling some 35 miles a day, he was well received by a Cherokee of mixed race in the last town of that tribe. Then, he endured a series of problems. He took a wrong turn and lost about five miles. He suffered from stomach pain. The land was difficult to travel because it was stony and hilly. Then he crossed more mountains.

It became cold and there was frost at night, but the lands were easier to travel. He passed through stands of chestnuts, oaks, hickories, some maple and a little under-brush. The path in general was easy. He saw two handsome brooks that apparently emptied into the Coosa River.[250]

On April 30, Willett arrived at the first Creek settlement. He was told that McGillivray was expected at the home of a nearby trader named Grierson. The meeting was all important. Would the two men be able to forge a relationship? At 6 p.m. McGillivray arrived. Willett gave him Washington's letter. Then, he attended a black drink ceremony, which he described as a religious activity, at the center of a town square.

The square consisted of four rows of seats, from 40 to 50 yards long, fronting each other, leaving an opening at each angle for entrance, Willett wrote in his journal. The seats were neatly matted with reed and covered with bark. They were 10 or 12 feet deep, rising higher in the rear than in the front, so as to give each person as he sat, an opportunity of seeing what was happening in the square. This structure, where public business was conducted, was large enough for several hundred people. Warriors held gourds, sang two long notes, then served each guest and other participants.

After delivering his introductory letter, Willett and McGillivray talked for a bit. They had a good supper and entertainment, then Willett went to bed, happy in being under the same roof with the man he had traveled so far to see. "Colonel McGillivray appears to be a man of an open, candid, generous mind, with a good judgment, and very tenacious memory," he wrote.[251]

The two men stayed at Grierson's for a couple of days. After traveling 10 miles, they arrived at Fish Pond Town and were entertained that evening with a dance by those who lived there. The next day they arrived at Hickory Ground.[252]

McGillivray quickly came to respect Willett and vice versa. The men who held the fate of the Creek Nation in their hands would get along well. "This officer during the War was particularly distinguished for enterprise and success, & has since filled respectable offices," McGillivray wrote to Panton. The chief found Willett to be as candid and benevolent as Pickens, possessing abilities but without "Show or parade." He believed Washington had appointed Willett because of "that puppy" Humphrey's failure to negotiate a treaty at Rock Landing.

He went on to tell Panton that Willett said Congress would not support Georgia's insistence on getting Creek land and that McGillivray and other chiefs should go to New York with him to settle the matter in person. That measure would certainly give the Creeks peace and security, "for a Treaty concluded on at N. York ratified with the signature of Washington and McGillivray would be the bond of Long Peace and revered by Americans to a very distant period…" he wrote. With such promising prospects held out to him, he did not hesitate to accept the invitation.[253]

McGillivray sent out a message for the chiefs of Lower Towns to meet at Ositchy on May 16 to discuss business. As was the custom, a number of sticks were sent to each town. One stick was thrown away each day, and when they were all gone, the meeting would be held. Meanwhile Willett toured the area, including the remnants of French Fort Toulouse and Little Tallassie, the apple grove where McGillivray was born five miles from Hickory Ground. Willett feasted on fish, venison, strawberries and mulberries.[254]

He and McGillivray, along with two servants, set out for Ositchy at 9 a.m. on May 12. The journey was critical. At 4 p.m. they had traveled 25 miles to an interpreter's house at Tuckabatchy. They spent the next couple of nights at the homes of traders.[255] At Coweta on the Chattahoochee River, they joined the residents who spent the night drinking a special mixture and having a grand time. [256]

On the 16th they arrived at Ositchy. The next day at 11 a.m. they joined chiefs at the town square for black drink.[257] Willett told them of Washington's invitation to New York where the president himself would sign a treaty. He assured them that the United States did not want any of the Creek lands. Washington would take measures to secure the territory for all of them, Willett said, and would punish all who acted contrary to any treaty that he and McGillivray would agree to.

Washington would also promote Creek trade by making goods available in a cheap and easy way and "to do all such things as will contribute to promote the welfare and happiness of your nation," he added.

Willett told the gathering that he was a messenger of peace and hoped the chiefs and warriors would go with him to the "council fire" in New York and form a treaty "which shall be strong as the hills, and lasting as the rivers."

He left for an hour so the chiefs could talk over his proposal. When he was called back in, Chief Hallowing King said that their fathers had instructed them that when any white people came to their country, they should take them by the hand and use them well. He said they had followed that advice and went to Rock Landing to treat but nothing was done. "…we were disappointed, and came back with sorrow," he said.

The chief noted that the road to New York was very long and the weather very hot, but that McGillivray and other chiefs would go with Willett. Whatever McGillivray decided to agree to in negotiations, he and the others would follow. He wished Willett well. "We will count the time our beloved chief is away, and when he comes back, we shall be very glad to see him, with a treaty that shall be as strong as the hills, and last as long as the rivers."[258]

Willett and McGillivray then traveled to Tuckabatchy where Willett delivered his talk to the men of that town. Chief White Lieutenant, of mixed race, said his people were willing to be at peace. The Creeks loved to stay at their homes and hunt but had gone to Rock Landing to negotiate a treaty. They had been made fools of and had not intended to go to any more treaty meetings.

"… but you have come a great way," he added, "and you speak very good: our beloved chief, and such other chiefs and warriors as may be chosen, will go with you, and we will agree to all they may do."

Willett and McGillivray returned to Hickory Ground and Willet wrote to Knox of the success in getting Creeks to the bargaining table in New York. He paid a messenger $40 to deliver the letter. He had accomplished his mission.

While he waited to embark on the trip North, Willett went five miles to see "a most superb ball play." Men women and children from nearby towns filled the paths on foot or horseback to attend. The night before there had been dancing and ceremonies.

At the ball game, there were about 80 players on each side. They had painted and decorated themselves as when going to war and stripped off their clothing. Some 300 yards was marked in a field with two poles at each end through which the ball must pass. The ball was tossed into the air and players with two rackets tried to catch it and throw it between the poles to get a point. The game usually consisted of 12 to 20 points.

"Large bets are made upon these occasions, and great strength agility, and dexterity are displayed" he wrote. "The whole of the present exhibition was grand and well conducted."

Throughout the game women supplied players with gourds and bottles filled with drink. "The day was fair," Willett noted, "and I returned home, much pleased with the amusement."[259]

He was also very pleased with the response he had gotten from the chiefs. The fact that he and McGillivray respected each other was a major factor in being able to call the mission a success. He had been the right man for Washington to send to the Creek Nation to try to avoid war.

CHAPTER 8

Chiefs Trek to New York

McGillivray's decision to go to New York did not come easily. Panton and Miro were both opposed to the trip because they feared Americans would gain too much power in the region.

Very much aware of their reservations about the trip, McGillivray knew he had to reassure them of the Creeks' intent to continue their relationship. Don't be distressed, McGillivray wrote to Panton. His trip should not in the least cause alarm or suspicion to those he had developed a relationship with, he told his friend and confidant. "My Conduct on every occasion has evinced to them the integrity & uprightness of my dispositions toward the engagements we Entered into & which now Subsists between my Nation & theirs." Further, Miro had encouraged him to make peace with the Americans and so should be in favor of his decision to go to New York.[260]

However, his allies were not convinced. Carlos Howard, a Spanish official in St. Augustine, wrote a very persuasive letter to McGillivray trying to convince him not to negotiate with the Americans. He stressed that Spain was the natural ally and protector of the Creeks. Trade was conducted without tariffs, he said, and Spain never asked for an inch of ground.

"The Americans will not act thus," Howard wrote. "They are an industrious people, stingy and commercial, although weak and still lacking in strength; therefore, they will aspire to enrich themselves with Indian trade; but this they cannot do without raising considerably the current price of the merchandise that you need. Very little of such merchandise is manufactured in

America; hence it must be imported and a tariff must be paid; to this must be added the increased cost of transporting by land to the Indian borders."

Howard warned that without the support of Spain, the Creeks risked losing even more land to the Americans. "Turn your eyes toward the north; reflect on what those tribes were in past times, and realize what they are today," he wrote. "The English and the French were in truth the first usurpers, but the Americans have already begun to imitate them, and will continue to do so until they have reduced the Creeks to the same level in which are now those who were once powerful, their now almost annihilated northern brothers.

"Do not imagine, esteemed sir, that I even remotely wish that there should not be a permanent peace between your nation," he added. "And the United States: far be it from me to have such thoughts!" But, he said, he hoped that the United States would not attempt to destroy the connections that had existed for a long time between the Creek Nation and the Spaniards. He wanted to make sure that any treaty with the United States that McGillivray agreed to would not harm the Spanish or reduce their lucrative trade business.

A Spanish Baron, Don Josef Ignacio de Viar, in New York would be glad to assist in forwarding any propositions McGillivray might have to the court in Madrid, Howard said and urged him to take advantage of the contact. So Howard essentially wanted McGillivray to maintain his Spanish relationship while negotiating with the Americans.[261]

Georgia officials apparently had made an overture to make McGillivray a citizen and give him back his father's estates. But he decided against accepting the offer, although he did need the money. He felt that he was underpaid by Spain at the rate of an interpreter and that if it were not for the Panton-Leslie trading house he would literally die of hunger. Repeatedly, McGillivray had requested, without success, the necessity of being paid more money.[262]

Meanwhile, Georgians believed that war was at hand. The *New York Weekly Museum* published a story datelined Augusta May 1, 1790, noting that although McGillivray was inclined to bring peace to the state, no person in the nation had been appointed to negotiate with him. They feared the truce was up.[263]

The state did not know of the plan being considered by Knox and Washington to invite McGillivray to New York to negotiate directly with them. In fact, as decided, the plan was kept secret so Georgia would not interfere in negotiations. Knox had won the battle over whether the federal government or states had the right to deal with Indians.

Interestingly, with war looming, McGillivray corresponded with Georgia officials. The *New York Daily Gazette* published a letter from McGillivray to Georgia Governor Edward Telfair. McGillivray had written on March 30, 1790, that since Rock Landing had failed to produce a treaty, he would not give up lands his warriors had taken from settlers.

"We are willing to conclude a peace with you, but you must not expect extraordinary concessions from us," he wrote. McGillivray added that in order to avoid more bloodshed he would be willing to treat on grounds of mutual agreement. It would be best, he said, if negotiations were managed by the nation.[264]

So, McGillivray shared the view of Knox and Washington that Indian issues should be the role of the federal government. But although McGillivray agreed to go to New York, he did so with reservations and questioned Washington's motivation. Unfortunately, he doubted that the president was willing to treat with him on principles of justice and humanity, which was exactly what Washington and Knox were trying to achieve.

Rather, he thought that the president's true feeling was to restrain the malevolence of the northern and eastern states against the southern. The powerful chief would much prefer to conclude negotiations on his own land but believed that it would be better for the Creek interests and those of their allies for him to go to New York. Spain still could protect her possessions and if she would do her part, he would do his.

McGillivray was faced with a Creek financial crisis. They desperately needed more money. "An expenditure of 15 to 20,000 pesos annually would get the most effective services of the red warriors," he wrote to Panton, "worth more than ten regiments of whites in this sort of warfare."[265]

Spanish officials did not entirely trust McGillivray. When they learned of the trip they sent a messenger to New York with money to supposedly buy flour but in reality to hinder the negotiations with the Creeks. The Spanish agent would try to spy on McGillivray.[266]

Ultimately, and believing there was little choice, McGillivray trusted his instincts and on Tuesday, the 1st of June, 1790, at 11 o'clock in the morning, he set out with Willett from Little Tallassie for the trip to New York. The group included McGillivray's young nephew and two servants, with eight warriors belonging to the Upper Creeks, and Willett's servant, John. They led several spare horses.

Through the Creek Nation, chiefs met them along the way. "I have now passed all the Indian settlements, and shall only observe, that the inhabitants of the countries appear very happy; and while the red and white alternately blend in their countenances, health and fragrance breathe around," Willett wrote.[267]

The 1,000-mile journey was marked by much uncertainty. The *New York Daily Gazette* reported that on June 7, Governor Telfair, who did not know of the planned New York meeting, reported to both houses of the state legislature that events presented a situation of necessary action. He said that three companies of Federal troops then present in Georgia caused him anxiety for the security of the frontier settlers because the soldiers were inadequate to defend the state. However, apparently referring to the truce, he said that the Creeks invariably preferred the most amicable disposition towards the citizens of the state ever since he had governed.

Negotiations could be successful, the optimistic new governor believed. Referring to earlier resolutions the General Assembly had passed in 1789, Telfair ordered that every means in the power of the state be taken to restore peace and harmony between Georgia citizens and the Creek Indians.[268]

Fortunately, the chiefs traveled without harm. Angry American settlers could have attacked them since they were venturing into no-man's land. Willett recorded on June 18 that 26 Indians rode in three wagons and four on horseback, as well as McGillivray, his nephew, two servants, the interpreter and Willet's servant. Willet rode in a sulky.[269]

At one settlement, a Mrs. Brown visited McGillivray. She had been a prisoner of the Creeks, captured with several of her children by warriors who killed her husband. McGillivray had freed her.[270]

Through Georgia and the Carolinas people were amazed at the scene of the peaceful entourage.[271] The Creeks arrived at Richmond on July 6 and stayed for three days. "...we were treated with the greatest attention," Willett wrote. "On the 8th, colonel M'Gillivray and myself dined in the academy with the governor, council, judges, a number of the gentlemen of the bar, and other persons of distinction."

McGillivray must have been amazed at the welcoming reception that he and his chiefs received. At Fredericksburg they were entertained at the theatre and at a dinner with all of the chiefs. "Visited Mrs. Lewis, the sister of our president, and several others of his relations," he wrote. "Viewed the place in which he was bred, and the cottage in which his mother died."

After a week, they set out for Philadelphia and were met by a message from Pennsylvania officials, hoping that he would stop at Gray's Ferry. "After halting and refreshing, for two or three hours, we were escorted into the city. In the evening, returned to Gray's gardens, to see the exhibition there."[272]

The Creeks were greeted at Philadelphia with much celebration. They attended a religious service at Christ Church. Bells were rung, a federal salute was fired, and the infantry escorted the chiefs to the Indian Queen tavern, where lodgings were prepared for them. Many citizens assembled to see the largest body of Indians that had been there in many years.[273]

The next day was spent paying visits. "The Indians were shewn a great many curiosities in and about Philadelphia; visited, formally, by a committee from the society of Friends," Willett wrote.

At dawn on Tuesday the 20th, he and the Creeks left Philadelphia. They arrived at Elizabeth-town Point at 4 o'clock in the afternoon, from which just at dusk Willett set out for New York, in a rowboat. He landed at White-hall dock, between 9 and 10 o'clock at night. Then, he left at 2 a.m. to go back to Elizabeth-town Point. Arriving there at 6 o'clock in the morning, he found a sloop, which had been sent from New York, ready to transport the group to the city.[274]

He boarded the ferry with the Indians. Their arrival was no surprise. Northeastern newspapers had announced that the Creeks were on their way. One account announced that McGillivray and his chiefs would arrive at Gray's Ferry and then proceed to New York City in the afternoon.[275]

When they docked at Murray's wharf at about 2 o'clock in the afternoon they were welcomed by the St. Tammany Society dressed in their splendid attire and the emblems of their order. The Society was in two files, led by the Grand Sachem, who brought McGillivray ashore. The Creeks must have marveled at the grand reception. They marched in the center of the group through Wall Street. They sang a native tune accompanied by a band from the troops, having a very striking effect on the numerous spectators who crowded the streets and windows. When they came opposite Federal Hall, McGillivray and the chiefs saluted Congressmen standing in the front of the balcony who returned the gesture, reported the *New-York Daily Gazette*.[276]

McGillivray was dressed in a suit of plain scarlet and the other chiefs and warriors in their Creek clothes. What a wondrous occasion, McGillivray must have thought. Knox and Washington surely were pleased at the grand event.

The procession moved on to Secretary of War Knox's home where several of the Creeks smoked a peace pipe before proceeding to Washington's residence, where they were introduced to the president. Washington greeted them in a very handsome manner, congratulated them on their safe arrival, and expressed a hope that the talks would prove beneficial both to the United States and the Creek Nation.[277]

There was more celebration to come. New York Governor DeWitt Clinton met them and escorted them to the City Tavern, where they would lodge. Knox, along with Georgia senators and representatives, dined with them there. One of the chiefs gave a brief speech expressing his sense of the honor conferred on the Indians by the kind reception given to them in New York. The mood was festive. The following toasts were drunk:

1. To the President of the United States.
2. The Kings, headmen, warriors and the Creek nation.
3. May the visit of the chiefs result in the prosperity and happiness of their nation.

4. May it be the glory of the American empire, to exhibit the most perfect justice towards its Indian allies.

5. A strong and perpetual chain of friendship between the United States and the Creek nation.

6. Oblivion to all prejudices and resentments.

7. A strong and perpetual chain of friendship between the United States and the Creek nation – may the horrors of war give place to the blessings of peace throughout the world.[278]

The *New York Daily Gazette* praised the grand event, observing that the immense crowds of the day, comparable to Washington's inauguration, were orderly and the Creeks dignified. The chiefs and warriors appeared to be men of distinction, the story said.[279] Vice President John Adam's wife, Abigail, met McGillivray and described him as a man who "dresses in our own fashion speaks English like a Native & I should never suspect him to be of that Nation, as he is not very dark."[280]

The *Gazette* also published an account of the Creek Nation. The article informed readers that the Creeks called themselves Muskogees and were composed of various tribes, who, after tedious wars, thought it good policy to unite to support themselves against the Choctaws and others.

The story did not entirely support the Creek Nation, however, stating that the Indians inhabited a noble and fruitful country, where they would become civilized, more and more every day. But then the article predicted that they, or some other people, more civilized and powerful, would one day enjoy all the advantages of the Creek lands with the superior soil and climate.

"They are remarkably well shaped, are expert swimmers, and are a sprightly hardy race," the article continued:

They teach their horses to swim in a very extraordinary manner, and find great use therein, in their war parties. They have abundance of tame cattle and swine, turkies, ducks, and poultry; they cultivate tobacco, rice, Indian corn, potatoes, beans, peas, cabbage, etc.

Their country abounds with melons, peaches, strawberries, plumbs, grapes, and some other fruits.

To strangers they seem hospitable, nay, liberally kind to excess, even to white men – when any above the rank of a trader visits them. With those they are punctual, and honest in their dealings; and they afford them protection from all insults. Many of the nations are addicted to trade as principals, or as factors for the London company, who are allowed by the Spaniards a free trade with them, in a stipulated number of ships from London annually.

Their women are handsome; and, considering their state of civilization, many of them are very cleanly. They are exceedingly attentive to strangers, whom they serve with excellent provision, well cooked, which are always accompanied with a bottle of chrystaline bear's oil, and another of virgin honey, full as pure.

Their country, or what they claim, is bounded northward, by nearly the 34th degree of latitude and extends from the Tombecklee or Mobelle river, to the Atlantic ocean. It is well watered by many navigable streams, leading to bays and harbours, which will become of great importance in peace and war; and is abundant in deer, bears, wild turkies, and small game.

The men value themselves on being good hunters, fishermen, and warriors, so much that their women still do most of the work of the field, which in this fine country and climate, is not very laborious. They are, however, adopting the use of black slaves.[281]

So, the *Gazette* readers became well informed about the Creeks, in the city to negotiate with the Washington administration for lasting peace.

CHAPTER 9

TREATY TALKS

McGillivray was sick in New York, which delayed treaty negotiations for a couple of weeks.[282] "The serious illness which has troubled me ever since my arrival has prevented me until now, from replying to the subjects suggested that you put in my hands in Philadelphia," he wrote to Spanish official Carlos Howard.[283]

Newspapers reported that McGillivray heavily drank while in the city.[284] There was plenty of opportunity for that. Knox and Jefferson took McGillivray to meet with foreign dignitaries. Several days later the Creek chiefs reviewed the city's troops with Washington, Knox, and New York Governor Clinton, then dined with Knox and his family.[285] Other evenings were spent at banquets with Washington, congressmen and other officials. Peace pipes were smoked, and arms locked in unity.[286] They were entertained aboard the *America* and the St. Tammany's Society held another banquet for them. McGillivray's illness then could have been from hangovers or from the chronic ailments which had plagued him his entire adult life.[287] McGillivray stayed at Knox's house for much of the time while the chiefs camped nearby.[288]

Congress passed legislation aimed at easing tensions between the parties. The day after the Creeks arrived in New York, Washington signed into law two acts that appropriated $20,000 to pay the cost of negotiating the treaty to promote peace and that required a license to carry-on trade with the Indians. Also, any sale of Indian land would now have to be under the authority of the United States.

Washington asked Secretary of State Jefferson what effect the new laws would have on negotiations. Jefferson responded that since McGillivray with Panton, Leslie & Company had a monopoly of commerce of the Creek Nation, they had a right to import their goods duty free; that trade agreement was the principal source of McGillivray's power. Therefore, the chief would be unwilling to enter into a treaty with the United States unless he could be assured that his current trade relationship would continue. Jefferson was unsure of how that could be done consistently with federal laws while avoiding complaints from Americans who would wish to participate in Creek trade.

United States citizens are not allowed to trade with the Creeks, Jefferson added. He suggested that duty-free trade by a limited number of licenses approved by the president would help solve the problem.[289] That stand would help resolve the trade issue which could not be ignored.

During the day, Knox and Jefferson handled negotiations for the United States and McGillivray spoke for the Creeks. Washington wanted the talks to be informal. No record was made of the them.[290] But correspondence and reports by the key negotiators provide much detail.

The Spanish were concerned about the effect on their holdings if the Creeks agreed to a deal with the United States. Their spy acting under the cover of buying flour was to try to influence negotiations. Washington learned of the plot and had the Spaniard followed so that he could not carry out his mission.[291]

However, McGillivray had promised to meet with a Spanish agent.[292] And he did. The Spaniard, Josef Ygnacio de Viar, wrote to his fellow officials, "In spite of the fact that these people have guarded him closely, and that he has been ill for a few days at the home of General Knox, where he has lodged since his arrival, we have been able to speak to him occasionally, taking advantage of all opportunities that have presented themselves. Up to the present he has appeared to be attached to us, but time will tell."[293]

One special occasion during the days of negotiating was the viewing of a portrait of Washington by the prominent artist John Trumbull. The artist attended the event and wrote that Washington was curious to see how the Creeks would react to the portrait.

Washington had directed Trumbull to place the picture in advantageous light, facing the entrance to the room. He had invited several of the Creek chiefs to dine with him. After dinner the president, dressed in full uniform, led the way to the room where the painting hung.

When the door was thrown open, the Indians were startled to see another 'Great Father' standing in the room. For a time, they were mute with astonishment.

"At length one of the chiefs advanced towards the picture, and slowly stretched out his hand to touch it, and was still more astonished to feel, instead of a round object, a flat surface, cold to the touch," Trumbull wrote.

The chief quickly backed up and exclaimed "Ugh!" Another chief approached the painting and placed one hand on the surface and the other behind and was astounded to realize that his hands almost met.

Trumbull had hoped to paint portraits of some of the chiefs, who possessed a dignity of manner, form, countenance and expressions he felt worthy of Roman senators. But he found it impractical because they thought the painting was magic since the smooth flat surface so closely resembled the real man. He did however sketch several of them secretly."[294]

The incident was a dramatic illustration of the differences in the two cultures trying to reach an agreement to save the Creek Nation. There were many problems that confronted McGillivray and Knox. Creek trade complicated the situation so even if boundaries were drawn, there was the question of who could cross them and swap goods. McGillivray was bound by a treaty from 1784 with the Spanish, which he could not honorably breach.[295]

McGillivray was very much aware of his obligations to the Spanish. In his letter to Howard from New York, he said Leslie had good reason for stressing that Spain was the natural protector of the Southern Indians. "This is not only my opinion but also the general one of those who are fairly well informed about our situation;" he wrote, "all consideration of a sane policy should dispose her (Spain) to such a protection. It is of equal importance for the interests of the Indian Nations that they be closely connected with Spain…"[296]

A crucial matter was the question of United States sovereignty over the Creeks. McGillivray held out for an agreement that would limit sovereignty to parts of the Creek Nation that were within boundaries of the United States.[297]

So, what would be designated as Creek country? One proposal was that the Creeks would get what is now Alabama, north Florida, Mississippi and part of Tennessee. However, Washington's goal of "civilizing" the Creeks would require them to have much less land because they would farm instead of hunt.[298] Negotiators also had to deal with the issue of whether certain lands were under the possession of Spain or the United States. They decided that the United States would gain control north or east of a boundary to be determined, with land south or west of that line to be under Spanish protection. McGillivray would have to give up part of the land claimed for Georgia so that the Creeks could keep good hunting grounds elsewhere.[299]

Despite the daunting task of many details to work out, Washington notified the Senate on August 4, 1790, that negotiations were progressing, although trade was an issue that still had to be worked out. He noted that the Creeks traded through Panton, Leslie & Company in ports held by the Spanish. So, their trade involved two foreign powers, England and Spain, he wrote.

Therefore, it was important to form new channels for Creek commerce through the United States. But that would require time, he said, because the present arrangements could not be suddenly broken without violating faith and morals.

He said a secret article of the treaty should be drawn up similar to one that he submitted. The document he enclosed stated that citizens of the United States could carry out Creek trade through the ports no later than August of 1792. The secret article was probably McGillivray's idea to protect his relationship with Spain. "In the meantime the said commerce may be carried on through its present channels, and according to its present regulations," the article stated.

McGillivray said after much debate that he agreed to defer changing trade partners for two years. "...it seemed to me the best way to escape this article, the most difficult point to adjust," he later wrote to the Spaniards.

These key players in the negotiations certainly understood that since Creek trade was currently being carried on mostly through Spanish territories, war or prohibitions by the Spanish government could hinder commerce. In the event that such obstructions did happen, it would then be lawful for the president of the United States to designate persons who could transport through United States territories to the Creek Nation any quantity of goods and merchandise up to $60,000 in any one year. That trade would be free of duties or impositions but subject to regulations to guard against abuse. So, Washington addressed the issue of Creek trade head on, but secretly. 300

Another major issue in negotiations was what to do about the disputed Oconee lands that Georgia claimed and had divided up among its settlers. "It occupied us several days, because the

Georgians and other interested persons insisted that the cessions made to them should be confirmed on the part of our nation," McGillivray wrote. "These lands had been alienated and populated and could not be restored except by force, and force could not be employed against the citizens, nor their blood shed." [301]

Jefferson said in a memo that Yazoo Companies' claims to the land were illegal because Georgia had in effect given that land to the United States when joining the union. Washington's personal secretary, Tobias Lear, wrote a message for the president to give to the Senate, which reflected Washington's thinking. Creeks were willing to give up some of the Oconee land, Lear wrote. But they absolutely refused to cede certain lands to the eastward of a new temporary line to be drawn from the forks of the Oconee and Ockmulgee rivers to the St. Mary's River. That highly disputed swath was in the Galphinton Treaty of 1785 that McGillivray had strenuously opposed.

That land was considered to be generally barren and impracticable, with the exception of some swamps on the margin of the rivers which, under improvement, would make rice paddies. However, most Creeks treasured it as their most valuable winter hunting grounds and had always refused to relinquish it.[302]

McGillivray came to realize that he had little choice. "I agreed that an arbitrary line should be drawn on the Oconee River for which the United States should make us immediately a compensation of ten thousand dollars in merchandise" he wrote, "and two thousand dollars annually; the United States surrendering all claims up to the new Georgian line, from the branch of the Alatamaya to the source of the St. Marys River and its various springs, the old British boundary over that river being included, and the United States being a guarantor of all future usurpations on the part of their citizens."[303]

Washington notified the Senate on August 6, 1790, that further progress had been made in resolving issues and the stage was set for a final agreement. "It therefore becomes necessary that a proper Person be appointed and authorized to Treat with these Chiefs, and to conclude a Treaty with them, " he wrote. "For this Purpose I nominate to you Henry Knox."[304]

Knox did carefully go over each word in the draft and made some edits to make sure every detail furthered the intent of justice, policy and humanity of the undertaking. He submitted the final treaty to interpreter Joseph Cornell who swore on oath before New York Chief Justice Richard Morris that he would truthfully translate the treaty to the Creek chiefs.[305]

Knox wrote a speech, which reflected the noble intentions that he was poised to get the federal government to adopt, that he delivered to the Creek chiefs:

> It having pleased the great master of breath to put into your hearts to repair to the President of the United States in order to conclude a perpetual treaty of peace and friendship with the United States – I rejoice that we have come to a final agreement on that subject.
>
> Both parties on the frontiers will now rejoice in all the blessings of life, and none shall make them afraid.
>
> The boundary between the white people and your nation will be fixed in such manner, that it cannot be mistaken or misunderstood.
>
> For the land you have relinquished you will receive an adequate compensation for the comfort of yourselves & children.
>
> The United States will be your steady and firm friends, and will be ever ready to promote your happiness – impress

upon your brethren and whole nation love and attachment to the citizens of the United States.

If any event should turn up which should look as if the United States had forgotten these sentiments, regard it not – they [sic] United States are just and true, and will never depart from their promises [sic]– whenever you think yourselves aggrieved ask an explanation and it shall be given you.

At the same time guard the conduct your rash young men and prevent their injuring any of the white people on the frontiers as we are all members of one great family, and their caust [sic] must be the cause of the United States – we will guard the conduct of ours and punish all who shall deserve it.

We will now proceed to read, sign, and seal the instrument of our future peace and friendship; and may the supreme principle of the universe render it perpetual.[306]

That evening, the Creeks celebrated the treaty that they hoped would save their nation by building a great bonfire and dancing around it whooping, singing and yelling to express their pleasure.[307]

The next day, Knox wrote to Washington that he, McGillivray and the Creek chiefs had signed a treaty. He said McGillivray also had signed secret articles on behalf of himself and the Creek Nation.

After the failure of Rock Landing, it was proper that the United States government proceed to establish a peace and avoid more bloodshed, Knox said. He revealed that in negotiations, his strategy had been to make the Creeks realize the danger of failing to reach an agreement. The United States would declare war and bring down the Creek Nation.

Those assurances had been conveyed to them by Willett, he said, and "the chiefs came with that confidence in the justice of the General Government which its fame has justly instanced, and which it will be its glory to preserve unsullied."[308]

Washington was pleased and wrote to the Senate that he was submitting the treaty subject to the ratification of himself as president with the advice and consent of the Senate. The document will bring peace and prosperity to the southern frontier, he proudly proclaimed. The consequence would be to firmly attach the Creeks and neighboring tribes to the interests of the United States.

He went on to say that he hoped Georgia would be satisfied because the Creeks had agreed to give up some of the Oconee land claimed by the state. Although the most valuable of the disputed land was included, Georgia's claim from the Galphinston Treaty of the land eastward of the Oconee and Ockmulgee to the St. Mary's was a tract that the Creeks in New York absolutely refused to yield. Washington noted again that the barren land was only good for growing rice and providing timber for building of ships.[309]

The drama was not over. The president's message and the treaty were read and submitted for consideration. On Monday, August 9, 1790, a motion to refer the document to a select committee was defeated by two votes and a motion to allow the statements of reasons for dissent was voted down. The treaty would have to be approved by a two-thirds majority.

The final treaty to be voted on declared that there would be perpetual peace and friendship between all the citizens of the United States of America and all individuals, towns and tribes of the Creek Nation. Creeks would not be party to any treaty by states or individuals.

Importantly, the Creek Nation would be considered within the limits and protection of the United States and no other sovereign. Spain, then, would lose control over the Creeks within United States boundaries.

Creeks would regain part of the disputed Oconee land, the prized hunting grounds on the Altamaha. Georgia would get much of the land the state had claimed and settled, but the Creeks would be paid $1,500 annually as compensation and the United States would guarantee their lands to the west and south of the boundary.

No one except Indians could settle on any of the Creek lands, and if they did the Creeks could punish them as they pleased. Also, anyone entering Creek lands would have to have a passport from an authorized official.[310]

The treaty seemed to be a remarkable agreement in the face of so many concerns. But not everyone was satisfied. Some Georgia officials were outraged that the federal government would give away their land. McGillivray, however, was relieved that the treaty "signed the death sentence of the Company of the Yazoo."[311]

The treaty also stated that the United States would help the Creek Nation achieve a greater degree of civilization, and to become herdsmen and cultivators, instead of remaining as hunters. The United States would furnish domestic animals and farm implements, as well as agents to act as interpreters.

In addition, the treaty included six secret articles that were only signed by McGillivray for the Creeks, and Knox, Jefferson and Washington for the United States. The one that addressed the thorny issue of Creek trade was among them. The proposed solution of Creeks continuing trade through Panton, Leslie and the Spanish for two years was adopted. McGillivray would be given the rank of Brigadier General and paid $1,200 a year. And McGillivray would commit to cultivating friendship between the United States and the Creek Nation. Each chief would be given a great medal with proper ornaments along with $100 a year.

The United States also would educate and clothe up to four Creek youth at any one time.[312]

Two days later, on August 11, 1790, the day before the Senate ratified the treaty, McGillivray wrote a lengthy letter to Spanish official Howard revealing how he felt about the agreement. He reassured Howard that he would not harm the Creek Nation's relationship with Spain and said he had sought advice from Spanish Governor Miro and other officials. But he also said the treaty with Spain had never been ratified and that goods had sometimes been scarce and sent with reluctance. Still, the trade arrangement had been very beneficial to the Creeks, he conceded.

"For this we are duly grateful; nevertheless, having reflected on everything maturely, I feel justified in concluding a peace with the United States, although it is not equal to our claims and desires," McGillivray stated. His refusal to agree to American propositions at Rock Landing the previous September had come close to causing very serious consequences, including an outright war, he acknowledged. That failure was considered by Washington as an insult to the United States, McGillivray wrote, despite the fact that the proceedings of the Georgians had been generally condemned.

If he had not traveled to New York to negotiate, Congress undoubtedly would have declared war against the Creeks, he conceded, noting that the new government was entirely capable of complete success. McGillivray went on to write that he would have no guarantee that Spain would help the Creeks if the United States declared war. "These motives have led me to agree to the following articles of peace to end our disputes," he said, and gave insight into the negotiations.

The first stipulation required of the Creeks was an unqualified recognition of the sovereignty of the United States over them. He opposed that article. After much debate it was modified, he explained, to extend over those parts of the Creek Nation within the boundaries of the United States and it did not seem worthwhile to object needlessly to that point.

Another stipulation was directed toward taking Creek trade from its present source, he continued. "After much debate it was decided to defer the consideration of this point until the end of two years, and it seemed to me the best way to escape this article, the most difficult point to adjust," he wrote. That issue took several days of talks, McGillivray said, because the Georgians insisted that the cessions made to them should be confirmed on the part of the Creek Nation. Those lands had been settled and could not be restored except by force, and McGillivray said he did not want bloodshed of citizens.

McGillivray acknowledged that he agreed to the line on the Oconee River from the Altamaha to the source of the St. Mary's River and to the compensation of $10,000 in merchandise immediately and $2,000 annually. "...everything considered, I am thankful that it did not turn out worse," he confided.

He explained that he did not seek the return of his estates in Georgia and South Carolina but would ask the states for compensation. He tried to resist as much as he decently could the honorary badge of Brigadier General and finally, tired of being repeatedly pressed to accept it, he agreed.

"The foregoing is an exact compendium of my negotiations here, which I give with candor and without reserve, and I flatter myself that no part of the treaty can give just motive for suspecting that I failed to fulfill my obligations," he wrote. Further, McGillivray stressed that he must have a clear commitment from Spain to carry out the Pensacola Treaty of 1784 instead of what he called the current vague and ambiguous procedures.

He said that he had strongly protested the Yazoo Companies and that he had the word of the United States government that the companies would be broken up.[313] Spanish officials corresponded among themselves, reporting that McGillivray, Knox and Jefferson had visited with one of their representatives.[314]

McGillivray apparently had secretly kept the Spanish apprised of negotiations and details of the final treaty. Spanish agent Viar wrote the day the treaty was ratified by the House of Representatives, "Little do they suspect that I know its contents."[315] Whatever agreement McGillivray would reach with the United States, he knew he could ill afford to severe ties with Spain.

On August 12, 1790, the Senate ratified the treaty and passed it into law on a vote of 15 to 4. Two of the nay votes were from Georgia senators.[316] Their negative votes were to be expected and Washington, Knox and Jefferson could not have hoped for a better outcome.

A signing ceremony was scheduled for the next day. Washington issued a proclamation stating that the treaty of peace and friendship between the United States and the Creek Nation had been ratified and ordered that it be published. "…and I do hereby enjoin and require all officers of the United States, civil and military, and all other citizens and inhabitants thereof, faithfully to observe and fulfill the same," the president stated.[317]

At noon on August 13, 1790, a large crowd of officials, Creek chiefs and citizens gathered at Federal Hall. Martha Washington and two grandchildren were there. Vice president John Adams and his wife, Abagail, joined the assembly along with the governor as well as congressmen and their wives.[318]

McGillivray was dressed in a blue and red military uniform while the chiefs wore their most beautiful regalia.[319] Their entrance was dramatic as they shrieked and yelled, then dignified Washington, dressed in purple satin, followed by Knox and war department clerks entered the hall.

It was a grand affair, as reported in the *Pennsylvania Pack and Daily Advertiser*:

New York, August 14 – Yesterday the treaty of peace and friendship between the United States and the Creek nation was solemnly ratified by the contracting parties, in Federal Hall, in the presence of a large assembly of citizens. The vice-president of the United States – the great officers of state – his excellency the governor – and of several members of both houses of Congress.

At 12 o'clock the President of the United States, and his suite – general Knox, the commissioner; the clerks of the department of the secretary of war; colonel M'Gillivray, and the kings, chiefs and warriors of the Creek nation being assembled, the treaty was read by the secretary of the president of the United States.

The president then addressed colonel M'Gillivray, the kings, chiefs and warriors; he said that he thought the treaty just and equal; and stated the mutual duties of the contracting parties; which address was communicated sentence after sentence, by Mr. Cornell, sworn interpreter, to all of which the Creeks gave an audible assent.

The president signed the treaty after which he presented a string of beads as a token of perpetual peace, and a paper of tobacco to smoke in remembrance of it: Mr. M'Gillivray rose, made a short reply to the president, and received the tokens.

This was succeeded by the shake of peace every one of the Creeks passing this friendly salute with the president; a song of peace, performed by the Creeks, concluded this highly interesting, solemn and dignified transaction.[320]

Only 24 of the chiefs signed the treaty. Accounts indicate that there were 27 to 30 chiefs in New York. A few might have been ill, Knox said.[321]

Knox later reported that the expenses of the Treaty of New York added up to $20,583 and presents afterward cost $22,279.[322] That sum, he said, was substantially less than the cost of war and would uphold the high ideals of the new government.

The St. Andrews Society of New York state elected McGillivray an honorary member at its quarterly meeting at the City Tavern. They invited the head of the Creek Nation to join them in celebration of the occasion with songs and food.[323]

The Creeks had been in New York for three weeks.[324] After festivities, they left for home escorted by lieutenant Caleb Swan. McGillivray left behind his young nephew who would be under the charge of Knox so the boy could get a good education. The Spanish were concerned that McGillivray therefore was under the spell of the United States. McGillivray assured them that was not the case, that he was just doing what was in the boy's best interest. Indeed, he would gladly allow another nephew to be raised by Spaniards except that the youngster would not learn English.[325]

McGillivray deliberated on the way home. Though he had avoided war, he was concerned that he would lose the all-important Spanish support, which was critical since Spain's territories abutted the Creek Nation.

He wrote words of reassurance to Florida official Quesada. "…You may be assured that no Stipulations or Articles of it any way Clash with or tends to Militate against those we have Subsisting with Spain & you may farther read on my best exertions to promote & Maintain the good Harmony & Friendship that Subsists at Present between our Nation & the Kings Provinces of the Floridas & Louisiana, which assurances I have repeated to the Gentlemen who you did me the honor to Send."[326]

After sailing to the St. Mary's, the Creeks continued the long journey by horseback.[327] The trip took its toll on McGillivray.

CHAPTER 10

PROMISES FAIL

On his way home, McGillivray was sick and exhausted. He wrote to the governor of East Florida, Juan Quesada, that he was too ill to accept an invitation to visit him at St. Augustine.

"Our Journey to New York proved tedious & fatiguing, & was on My arrival there seized with a Violent indisposition which held me a long time, & before I was perfectly recovered I embark for this place," he wrote. Traveling even further in the oppressive heat, he said, would greatly lengthen the trip and make him even more ill. McGillivray assured Quesada that the Treaty of New York would not harm his relationship with Spain and that the governor could rely on his friendship.[328]

Also, while on the journey home, McGillivray wrote to John Leslie, of Panton, Leslie & Company and said Yazoo Company officials wanted him to accept land grants so that he would be a partner with them. McGillivray complained that the company was using his name to sell land without paying him and ignoring an act by Congress prohibiting schemes of land speculators. So, his optimism that Yazoo had been taken care of by the Treaty of New York was short lived.[329]

Distrust was widespread. Spanish officials feared that the Americans would have priority with McGillivray at their expense. Carlos Howard, the aide in St. Augustine, reported to Quesada that McGillivray had told him at a meeting at St. Mary's River that the Georgians erroneously thought the treaty severed Creek connections with Spain and that he would only allow Americans to enter his nation to trade. To counter that interpretation of the Treaty of New York, Howard said, McGillivray had promised that he would require any trader to obtain a permit from him and that he would confiscate all goods brought by anyone without a license. Howard went on to say that Americans directly or indirectly were trying to prejudice Creeks against the Spanish.

Howard was also suspicious of Swan accompanying McGillivray from New York. He doubted that the captain's true mission was to fill a post of superintendent of Indian affairs. Instead, he was convinced that Swan was sent to the Creek Nation to inspire McGillivray and his people to gain affection for the United States and to destroy their attachment to the Spaniards.[330]

In other letters, Spanish officials wondered about the ramifications of the treaty.[331] Many of the Creek chiefs were themselves unhappy with provisions of the treaty, as was Panton, who felt deceived. He and the Spaniards had to wait for several months to get a complete copy of the document, which they wanted the Creeks to ignore. Rumors flowed freely, claiming that McGillivray was getting several times the actual amount of money he was promised. The Spanish also thought McGillivray had agreed to American sovereignty and United States trade with the Creeks. Therefore, the Spanish officials actively sought to make the Creeks unhappy with the treaty terms.[332]

Likewise, Georgia did not stand idly by after the treaty was ratified. Congressman James Jackson denounced it a few months later, as he had when the treaty came up for a vote in the Senate. He said the treaty had alarmed Georgians and had wrongfully given away three million acres of the state's land. Instead of recognizing the rights of Georgia, he claimed, the treaty had "given away her land, invited a savage of the Creek nation to the seat of Government, caressed him in a most extraordinary manner, and sent him home loaded with favors." The Georgia legislature agreed with Jackson and officially protested that the treaty violated the state's rights. The conflict caused by federalism would not go away. Georgians were outraged that the state did not get title to lands claimed under the Treaty of Shoulderbone and that McGillivray had been treated so well in New York despite years of violent confrontations with Georgia settlers. Not all colonists in the state agreed. One Georgian wrote to Washington that he was pleased that the goal was to teach the Creeks farming and that he would like to be considered for the job of helping them.[333]

But that gentleman was in the minority. Thousands of pioneers settled onto Creek lands, with no regard for boundaries set in the Treaty of New York. The high ideals and promises in the treaty were ignored, proving impossible to actually implement. The Georgia Legislature in January of 1791 refused to abide by Washington's executive order prohibiting settlement on Indian lands. They sold more than 15 million acres of land to the controversial Yazoo Companies.[334] Much of that land had been confirmed to the Creeks in the treaty. Most of the Georgia legislators owned shares in the land company. Yazoo failed to pay Georgia in gold and silver so the state rescinded grants, yet settlers came anyway. Knox sent federal troops, but historian Ellis noted, "It was like stopping a flood with a bucket of sponges."[335]

McGillivray thought he would have to go to war with Georgia and would be supported by the treaty. He wrote to Miro in February of 1791, that Georgians were encroaching but that he had the authority to stop them and the Yazoo Companies.[336]

He said he had asked to get his father's plantations returned but that Congress did not have the authority to do so and he accepted payment instead of $1,200 a year. He also wrote that he had refused the commission of Brigadier General and would honor his commission in the Spanish service instead. So, he tried to hedge his bets and keep from losing any protection for his people.[337]

In June of 1791, McGillivray wrote to Miro that settlers were ignoring the treaty. McGillivray believed that some 150 men planned to erect a fort and settlement at Muscle Shoals on the Cherokee River in what is now north Alabama. He sent out warriors to stop the intruders but did not find them. Dispatching his fighters was a clear indication that McGillivray was determined to protect his lands and would force the colonists out with violence if necessary. He said he might need Spain's help to keep the Georgians from encroaching on Creek land.[338]

As turmoil engulfed the Creek Nation with American whites grabbing land, William Bowles took advantage of the instability. He tried to get Creeks to oppose both the United States and Spain and to overthrow McGillivray. Panton called Bowles a mad dog, a pirate, whom any decent person would shoot down on sight. He offered one man a pension for life to kill him, but the plan was unsuccessful.[339]

Knox was surely disappointed that events prohibited peace but he didn't give up. He sent two men, Andrew Ellicott and his brother, Joseph, to run boundary lines between the Creek Nation and Georgia. "Since the boundary was established by the Treaty of New York, it is hoped that the Creeks will cooperate in drawing the line and will assist in maintaining peace on the southwestern frontier," Knox wrote.[340]

But McGillivray delayed, blaming Bowles for stirring up trouble.[341] Bowles was able to convince Lower Creeks who were unhappy with the Treaty of New York to trust him instead of McGillivray.[342] Outraged, McGillivray called him a liar and promised a reward of $300 for killing him, to no avail. He wrote to Panton that he had sent three warriors to kill Bowles, but the "Vagabond" was so well guarded that they failed.[343] However, he was convinced that it was just a matter of time before Bowles would be murdered when his lies became known. McGillivray's advisor Milfort met Bowles and wrote that he was "a man without honor and without honesty."[344]

McGillivray was at his lowest point, writing to Panton, "…I am absolutely worn down with the Life I have lived for ten years past." He was physically tormented by severe rheumatism and emotionally discouraged that some of his chiefs had turned against him. He said he would leave Little Tallassie and go to Mobile and New Orleans.[345]

McGillivray went to Pensacola, but the gout prevented him from going on to New Orleans to meet with Miro about problems in the region, so he wrote the Spanish official and urged Spain to rid the country of Bowles. He stressed that Bowles' influence was limited to a couple of Lower Creek chiefs.

At one point, he was so dispirited over the Lower Creeks' allegiance to Bowles that he declared he would no longer be chief. He did in fact move all of his possessions and slaves to his Little River estate, which was in Spanish territory. And Spanish officials noted that McGillivray was no longer powerful in leading the Creeks.[346] Later, however, his letters indicate that he did go back to Little Tallassie and continued to negotiate for his people.

In New York, Washington came to sadly realize that his efforts to enact an honorable approach to saving Indians might fail. On April 3, 1791, he wrote, "Until we can restrain the turbulence and disorderly conduct of our own borders, it will be in vain I fear to expect peace with the Indians – or that they will govern their own people better than we do ours." He blamed the white settlers and complained that "a lawless set of unprincipled wretches…can infringe the most solemn treaties, without receiving the punishment they so richly deserve." Scarcely anything short of a Chinese wall would restrain the land speculators and the encroachment of settlers upon the Indian Country, he ruefully observed.[347]

Knox agreed but estimated that it would take 50,000 troops and multiple forts to enforce the order and protect Indian territory.[348] Undeterred by Knox's estimation, the next day Washington wrote to Alexander Hamilton that it appeared war was imminent. Every measure was being taken to avoid battle with hostile tribes and to keep the Creeks in good temper, but he was thoroughly convinced that neither effort was effective. Any steps toward those goals were likely to be of short duration because the borders were being ignored. The states were continuing to overstep their role and interfere in matters, which belonged to the federal government.

Hamilton replied that if war resulted there was nothing to do but meet it with vigor and added that in his department provisions were adequate.[349]

Historian Ellis observed in *American Creation* that Washington felt that he personally had failed, "believing that his signature on the Treaty of New York was his pledge of honor as well as the solemn word of the United States government. Both were now being exposed as worthless."[350]

The good will of Washington, Knox and Jefferson was unsuccessful because white settlers outnumbered Indians, the United States could not protect Creek borders and peace with Indians had little true support in Congress.[351]

Also, the Spanish effort to sway Creeks against McGillivray was successful in some towns and a few chiefs came to believe that the Treaty of New York should not be enacted. McGillivray was losing control of his Creek Nation. He went to New Orleans, Mobile and Pensacola. Some claimed he had fled.[352]

Since the Treaty of New York did not live up to its promised peace, McGillivray had to get back in the good graces of Spain, promising that he would align with them instead of the

Americans. Though changing loyalties could be viewed as fickle, he actually had no choice.

The situation was critical and sadly McGillivray also had to contend with his debilitating health problems. A traveler through the south in 1791, John Pope, visited McGillivray and described the chief as looking 10 years older than his age because he was delicate and feeble, subject to headache and colic. Yet his temperament was placid and serene and at times quite joyous. Well educated, he had ample wit and humor, Pope wrote.

McGillivray proudly showed him gifts from Washington — a set of elegantly gilt bound books and a golden epaulet that the president had worn through the war. McGillivray said he prized the gifts more than rubies or gold. Perhaps he felt that his greatest achievement had been agreeing to the Treaty of New York. Pope noted that McGillivray was a gracious man, writing letters thanking his hosts in Richmond and Manchester for entertaining him on his way to New York. [353]

Despite the dismal outlook, Knox wrote to Georgia Governor Telfair on September 8, 1791, that the lines marking Creek territory were going to be run and that he hoped there would be no impediment to the immediate drawing of the boundaries.[354]

He ordered Mayor Henry Gaither to take troops to Georgia to prevent the incursion of small parties of violent Creek Indians. He gave Gaither a copy of the Treaty of New York and instructions to occupy a post at St. Mary's but to avoid offensive measures against the Creeks. He was to handle supplies and pay the Indians.[355]

But the lines would not be run. McGillivray wrote to Panton that the American commissioners could not guarantee the safety of his men in the face of bandits on the frontier. So, he would not send men to mark the boundaries.[356]

Even so, Washington and Knox lived up to their agreement to pay the Creeks, sending $2,900 in gold. Washington had sent an officer to deliver McGillivray his salary loaded on horses but one of the sacks broke going through the town of Okfuskee. The officer told the Indians gathered around that it was money for McGillivray, which made them very angry. They flew into a great rage and spread the word throughout the Creek Nation that their supreme chief was a traitor and that he should be killed. Milfort claimed they would have murdered McGillivray, but he convinced McGillivray to send his commission back to Washington and escape to Mobile and Pensacola.[357] So, even that act was disputed as the Creeks argued about how to distribute the money and McGillivray wrote Knox not to send any more.[358]

Historian Ellis aptly described the aftermath of the Treaty of New York. "In effect, less than two years after the passage of the Treaty of New York all the hopes and peaceful prospects it embodied had evaporated," he wrote. The relentless encroachment of Creek lands by white settlers was unstoppable, he observed, undoing the very principles of the Treaty of New York. McGillivray had to rely on the Spanish to supply weapons for fighting the intruders.

"Whatever opportunity had ever existed for a new direction in Indian policy that preserved a tribal presence east of the Mississippi was lost forever," Ellis concluded.[359]

McGillivray also had to contend with even more uncertainty. Miro was leaving his post as governor of Louisiana. McGillivray wished him well. In what he lamented as his last occasion to address a letter to him in that capacity, McGillivray wrote, "Accept therefore my warmest thanks & acknowledgements as well on my part Individually as in behalf of my Nation for the Many proofs You have given us of Your attention to our real Interest & happiness..."[360]

Miro's replacement might not be as supportive of the Creeks. However, McGillivray was relieved when the new governor, Baron de Carondelet, ordered one of his officers to take Bowles dead or alive. Carondelet said an armed boat with 20 soldiers would cruise the Florida coast near the Apalachee River in hopes of capturing Bowles.[361] The mission failed, and Bowles robbed Panton's store at St. Marks, taking all the goods and skins. Panton passionately pleaded for McGillivray's help in capturing the thief. His letter was a clear indication of the close ties he had forged with the Creeks and the obligation that they owed him:

> When you were all poor & naked I voluntarily relinquished ease & the pleasures of refined Society to live amongst you for no other end than that of administering to your wants. I have been the means of your closing sic your women & children for seventeen years past who must otherwise have gone naked. Many hundred of your people have I fed when they were Starving, & when you had enemies to Contend with, you all know that my exertions were forever in your favour, & for all these favours your people have Joined with a Scoundrel to destroy me. I demand Satisfaction from the Nation in General for this outrage; I do not expect that the Nation will be able to restore to me what I have lost, but I demand the Life of that Villain Bowls sic, who has been the Cause of all this mischief, or that he may be taken & delivered over to the Spanish Garrison, in order that he be tried according to the Laws he has so wickedly broke through.

Then, Panton angrily wrote to the chiefs of the Lower Towns who had become loyal to Bowles and helped him rob the store yet addressing them as friends and brothers. He told them he had been honest with them, supplying their towns with goods and protecting them from enemies. And, he argued, they should be loyal to their great leader McGillivray:

> Brothers you have not acted right, but I do not blame you so much as I do your adviser, nor is it yet too late to regain my Good opinion; Mr. McGillivray Served you faithfully, & whoever tells you the Contrary is a liar & the Truth is not in him; I advise you to go to him and apologize for your behavior, he is generous & will forgive you.

> As to me and what you have done to me I must have Satisfaction & the only Satisfaction that I wish or seek for is the punishment of that Villain that Prince of Liars Bowles, whom you must bring here dead or alive; and then the Talk will be Straight between us.[362]

The Creek Nation had become so divided that the all-important trade economy was threatened. As for McGillivray, perhaps he did flee. He spent many days in New Orleans and Pensacola, ill much of the time. One of his letters indicated more attention to his illness than to politics. He wrote to O'Neill in January 1792, that he had scalded his leg with hot water, adding to his illness of rheumatism and fever which would confine him for a month.[363]

That lack of focus drew the attention of the Spanish. In the spring, the new Spanish governor in New Orleans, Carondelet, wrote Panton that he was surprised at the indifference and slowness of McGillivray in stopping Bowles. He urged Panton to help prevent the enactment of the Treaty of New York, which he said was harmful to Spain as well as to Panton. He asked Panton to convince McGillivray to ignore the treaty or risk losing his pension.

Carondelet further said that if Americans continued to encroach on Creek lands, that he not only would supply the

Creeks with arms and ammunition but would get other tribes to help.

Fortunately for McGillivray, Bowles made the mistake of going to New Orleans because he thought Carondelet would recognize his authority over the Creeks and unite against the Americans. Instead, Carondelet had him arrested and sent to Spain.[364] McGillivray wrote to Carondelet in April that he was pleased to hear that Bowles was "in the Situation to be rewarded for his daring Villainies."[365]

However, Carondelet also sought to usurp power from McGillivray, whom he blamed for siding with the Americans. He sent an agent, Pedro Olivier, to Little Tallassie to try to stop McGillivray from enacting the Treaty of New York. Olivier failed at a meeting to convince the chiefs to go against McGillivray who astutely explained that the previous Spanish governor had favored the treaty.[366]

It's not clear what his motive was, but McGillivray later arranged more meetings throughout Creek country at which Panton and Olivier forbid running the line between them and Georgia. They stressed that American traders should not be allowed on Creek land.[367] Still, even though McGillivray was present at those meetings, Olivier notified Carondelet that he believed McGillivray was very much interested in fulfilling the treaty with Americans.[368]

All the while, McGillivray continued to suffer from illness and refrained from meeting American agents to mark boundaries. "A long attack from the Rheumatism & the exceeding great Rains & high waters prevented me from going to the Oconee River about running the line until Mr. Panton arrived here," he wrote to O'Neill in May 1792. Two weeks later, he wrote again to say that his constant companion rheumatism had made a fresh attack on him.[369]

United States agent James Seagrove was becoming impatient. He had been commissioned by Washington to aid in Creek affairs. He wrote to Knox that he was puzzled that McGillivray was indifferent to the turmoil in Creek country.

"I wish I may be deceived, but I fear you will not find him, in the end, the man you wish him to be," he wrote. "A man, to preserve his reputation, ought not to serve many masters; the General (McGillivray) has many, and I am convinced the United States are not the favorite."

A Spaniard or an Englishman is welcomed all through the Creek Nation, he said, but it is very dangerous for any person, known to belong to the United States to travel or be in that country. "I am sorry to find that no pains have ever been taken to remove that unjust prejudice," he wrote. [370]

Thus, the high ideals in the Treaty of New York failed to materialize. There were just too many factors in play to make it work. And McGillivray did have to serve many masters. Spanish officials and the Englishman Panton had their own interests at heart and were not going to bow to the American effort to control the region.

Yet, Washington strongly believed the United States could still be honorable in Indian affairs and treat the Creeks fairly. He addressed Congress in December 1792, urging that trade could improve Indian relations. Constant and plentiful supplies with a ready market for Indian commodities could improve the prospects for peace, he said. [371]

McGillivray couldn't afford to take a chance on the Americans. He decided in July 1792, to go to New Orleans to gain favor with Carondelet. The two men negotiated a treaty in which McGillivray promised to remain loyal and gave Spain land in Louisiana and West Florida. In return, Carondelet promised to provide guns and ammunition not only to defend Creek country but even to regain their encroached lands if Americans refused to leave by a time to be determined. He also increased McGillivray's pension by $1,500 a year, which would total $3,500 annually.[372] In effect, McGillivray had denounced the Treaty of New York. And McGillivray gave up his American salary as an indication that he would be loyal to the Spanish.[373]

On his way back home, McGillivray had to stop in Mobile for a while because he was gripped with a high fever. Despite having achieved a new treaty with Spain, he could not feel at ease. He did not hesitate to continue trying to maintain relations with the Americans. When he finally returned to Little Tallassie, he wrote Seagrove and attributed the disturbances in the Creek Nation to Spanish interference. Then, he wrote to Knox and assured him that he was desperately trying to get the chiefs to comply with terms of the treaty, but that Spaniards were convincing them otherwise.[374]

His illness became worse and he confessed in a letter to Panton that he was suffering and unable to tend to business. Though he had much to do, the gout seized him and laid him up for nearly two months. "Every periodical attack grows more Severe & longer in Continuance," he lamented. "It now mounts from my feet to my knees, & am Still Confind to the fire side…" If not for his debilitating illness he would have gone to the Lower Towns for he was the only one who could convince the chiefs of his good intentions.[375]

McGillivray also complained of his illness to Carondelet. The Spanish official sympathized with him and offered a cure. "I am infinitely sorry that you are tormented so frequently with Rheumatism," he wrote in a December letter. A famous powder invented for the king might help. He offered to send a prescription on the understanding that it not be shown to any physician. It is unclear why he would forbid a doctor from seeing it.[376]

Apparently the "powder" was sent to McGillivray and he did take it. But instead of getting better, McGillivray's symptoms became much worse. Despite his illness, he continued to try to manage Creek affairs, writing later to Carondelet that he was taking steps to calm the situation between the Indians and Americans. He also continued his travels and undertook another visit to Panton. He became deathly ill on his way to Pensacola.

McGillivray managed to get to Panton's house. Dangerously ill, he was bedridden with gout and pneumonia. He was so sick that Panton said there was no hope of recovery and wrote to Carondelet to notify him of McGillivray's condition.[377]

McGillivray died of inflamed lungs and stomach gout at Panton's house on February 17, 1793, at 11 o'clock at night.[378] He was buried in Panton's garden with Masonic honors.[379] The Creeks who were with him wailed in sorrow.[380]

Rumors were widespread in the Creek Nation that the Spanish had poisoned their great leader. Milfort wrote to Carondelet that he feared for Olivier's life because the McGillivrays claimed Alexander had been poisoned.[381] The possibility of poisoning has never been ruled out.

"...it is very significant that Carondelet tells Alexander not to show his prescription of the 'powder' to any physician," writes Amos Wright in *The McGillivray and McIntosh Traders*. "Reflecting on this, it seems a strange request for the Governor of Louisiana to make." In his position, he would have nothing to fear from its revelation – unless the prescription was an overdose of mercury.

Mercury poisoning could have caused the pneumonia symptoms, historian Wright wrote. He also noted that Pensacola commander O'Neill wrote to Carondelet three days before McGillivray became ill on the trail and 12 days before he died and said, "They are now free from McGillivray's policies."[382]

Whether his death resulted from poison, syphilis, alcoholism or other ailments, of which there were many that had plagued him, McGillivray would not be replaced.

A lengthy obituary notice in *The Gentleman's Magazine* of London praised the great chief of the Creek Nation;

Feb. 17. At Pensacola, Mr. McGillivray, a Creek chief, very much lamented by those who knew him best. There happened to be at that time at Pensacola a numerous band of Creeks, who watched his illness with the most marked anxiety; and when his death was announced to them, and while they followed him to the grave, it is impossible for words to describe the loud screams of real woe which they vented in their unaffected grief. He was, by his father's side a Scotchman, of the respectable family of Drumnaglass, in Invernesshire. The vigour of his mind overcame the disadvantages of an education had in the wilds of America; and he was well acquainted with all the most useful European sciences. In the latter part of his life he composed, with great care, the history of several classes of the original inhabitants of America; and this he intended to present to Professor (William) Robertson, for publication in the next edition of his History (*The History of America*). The European and the American writer are no more; and the MSS of the latter, it is feared, have perished, for the Indians adhere to their custom of destroying whatever inanimate objects a dead friend most delighted in. It is only since Mr MacGillivray [sic] had influence amongst them, that they have suffered the slaves of a deceased master to live.[383]

American newspapers also printed obituary notices. "Died, in the Creek country, Colonel Alexander MGillivray sic, the celebrated chief of that nation, and an ally of the United States," reported *The Washington Spy*.[384]

Panton, ever the loyal friend to the Creek chief, wrote to McGillivray's father, Lachlan, in a letter dated April 10, 1794:

> Your son sir, was a man that I esteemed greatly. I was perfectly convinced that our regard for each other was mutual. It so happened that we had an interest in serving each other, which first brought us together, and the longer we were acquainted, the stronger was our friendship.

> ...I found him deserted by the British, without pay, without money, without friends, and without property, saving a few negroes, and he and his nation threatened with destruction by the Georgians, unless they agreed to ceded them the better part of their country. I had the good fortune to point out a mode by which he could save them all, and it succeeded beyond expectation....He died on the 17th February, 1793, of complicated disorders – inflamed lungs and the gout on his stomach. He was taken ill on the path coming from his cow-pen on Little River, where one of his wives, Joseph Curnell's daughter, resided, and died eight days after his arrival here. No pains, no attention, no cost was spared to save the life of my friend. But fate would have it otherwise, and he breathed his last in my arms.

> ...He died possessed of sixty negroes, three hundred head of cattle, with a large stock of horses.

> ...I advised, I supported, I pushed him on, to be the great man. Spaniards and Americans felt his weight, and this enabled him to haul me after him, so as to establish this house with more solid privileges than, without him, I should have attained. This being the case, if he had lived, I meant besides, what he was owing me, to have added considerably to his stock of negroes. What I intended to do for the father, I will do for his children. This ought not to operate against your making that ample provision for your

grandson, and his two sisters, which you have it in your power to make. They have lately lost their mother, so that they have no friends, poor things, but you and me. My heart bleeds for them, and what I can I will do. The boy, Aleck, is old enough to be sent to Scotland to school, which I intend to do next year, and then you will see him.[385]

McGillivray's sister, Sophia, had his body moved from Pensacola to Choctaw Bluff on the Alabama River near his Little River plantation and where his wife, who died several months later, would also be buried.[386]

His faithful followers would have been pleased at the historical perspective he left. In 1851, historian Albert James Pickett remembered him as a great man, though flawed. His death was a severe loss to Panton and the Spanish. The great chieftain's death, among the Creeks everywhere, produced deep sorrow and regret. He had long been their pride; the man who had elevated the Creek Nation and sustained it in troubled times now lay buried.

Like all other men, he had his faults. "He was ambitious, crafty, and rather unscrupulous; yet he possessed a good heart, and was polite and hospitable," Pickett wrote. "For ability and sagacity, the reader will admit that he had few superiors." Pickett called him the Talleyrand of Alabama.[387] Pickett was referring to Napoleon's skilled negotiator, French duke Charles Maurice de Talleyrand-Perigord, who unfortunately was suspected of being a traitor.

Pickett said McGillivray was a man of towering intellect and vast information, who ruled the Creek country for a quarter of a century[388] The historian wished he could defend the treachery and selfish aggrandizement of McGillivray's conduct, but could not. "However he may have been wronged by the Americans, he ought to have acted in good faith with them, after he had made the treaty with Washington. But McGillivray was like many ambitious and unscrupulous Americans of our day, who view politics as a trade."

In his defense, McGillivray had had many political balls to juggle. Washington could not keep Georgian settlers off Creek lands, Spain was offering to step in to protect her interests, so what was McGillivray to do? And Pickett praised the Creek chief for being a master of diplomacy. "He was almost unrivalled in intrigue," Pickett wrote, "and we doubt if Alabama has ever produced, or ever will produce, a man of greater ability."[389]

Present-day historian Ellis agreed that McGillivray was a capable and shrewd leader who was a master at handling the cards that were dealt to him. Though at times he had to be unscrupulous as a practical matter, Ellis noted that "he was incorruptible whenever the fate of the Creek Nation was at stake, and his combination of pure intelligence, diplomatic agility, and sheer audacity made him the most effective Indian leader of his time."[390]

EPILOGUE

For the rest of his life, George Washington lamented his inability to achieve justice for the Indians. In his farewell address in August 1796, he said, "I have thought much on this subject and anxiously wished that these various Indian tribes as well as their neighbours, the White People might enjoy in abundance all the good things which make life comfortable and happy."[391]

In the early 1800s, the federal government began moving Indians west of the Mississippi. By the end of 1850, the Creek Nation had come to an end and most of its people had been driven west of the Mississippi to Oklahoma. It was a fate that McGillivray had spent his life trying to prevent. In the south Alabama town of Atmore, a small reservation of the Poarch Band of Creek Indians remains the only remnant of the great Creek Nation still living within its ancestral lands.

But certainly, McGillivray would have been pleased to know that a Creek delegation from Oklahoma traveled to Washington, D.C. in 2015 for the installation of the 1790 Treaty of New York into a display at the new National Museum of the American Indian.

ACKNOWLEDGEMENTS

Historian and Pulitzer Prize winner Joseph J. Ellis wrote an essay "The McGillivray Moment" that convinced me that my project about Alexander McGillivray was definitely worthwhile.

McGillivray of the Creeks, a collection of McGillivray correspondence by John Walton Caughey, was invaluable. It is a work that is irreplaceable to any research on McGillivray. Aside from his masterful analysis of the issues facing McGillivray, Caughey provides translations of McGillivray letters to Spanish officials. I would have been lost without them.

The New York Public Library Milstein Microform Reading Room was a gold mine. Newspaper articles dating back to McGillivray's years provided many recorded details that made the era come alive. The staff was so helpful.

My dear friends Carol and Bill Nunnelley stayed interested in my project over many, many delightful dinners. Writers and editors themselves, they were always encouraging.

Many thanks to the team at Ebook Launch for actually getting my book into print. They are professional and quick to respond to any questions.

I am so fortunate to have a writer and fabulous editor as my husband, Nick. His help while I was researching and writing about Alexander McGillivray cannot be overstated. On a day to day basis he kept me going and eagerly went with me to do research and helped me find wonderful material at the New York Public Library.

ENDNOTES

Chapter 1

1 Michael D. Green, "Alexander McGillivray," *American Indian Leaders,* edited by R. David Edmunds, (University of Nebraska Press, Lincoln and London, 1980), p. 42.

2 Claudio Saunt, *A New Order of Things, Property, Power, and the Transformation of the Creek Indians, 1733-1816,* (Cambridge University Press, Cambridge, United Kingdom, 1999), p. 28.

3 Robbie Ethridge, *Creek Country, The Creek Indians and Their World,* (The University of North Carolina Press, 2003), p. 32.

4 Saunt, *A New Order of Things,* p. 18.

5 Albert James Pickett, *History of Alabama,* (River City Publishing, 2003), p. 76.

6 William Bartram, *The Travels of William Bartram,* p. 68.

7 Ethridge, *Creek Country,* p. 31.

8 Ibid., p. 31.

9 Henry Knox letter to George Washington, July 6, 1789, Founders Online, https://founders.archives.gov. (accessed December 5, 2017).

10 Saunt, *A New Order of Things,* p. 29, 35.

11 Ibid., p. 22

12 Ibid., p. 31.

13 William Bartram, *William Bartram on the Southeastern Indians,* (University of Nebraska, 1995). p. 113, 160.

14 David H. Corkran, *The Creek Frontier, 1540-1783*, (University of Oklahoma Press, 1967) p. 52.

15 Ibid., p. 51.

16 Ibid., p. 62.

17 Ibid., p. 83.

18 Pickett, *History of Alabama*, p. 422-423.

19 Amos Wright, *The McGillivray & McIntosh Traders on the Old Southwest Frontier, 1716-1815,* (New South Books, 2001), p. 69.

20 Saunt, *A New Order of Things*, p. 43.

21 Ibid., p. 44.

22 Corkran, *The Creek Frontier, 1540-1783*, p. 33.

23 John Walton Caughey, *McGillivray of the Creeks*, (University of Oklahoma Press, 1938; new material, University of South Carolina, 2007), p. 9.

24 Pickett, *History of Alabama*, p. 342.

25 Ibid., p. 342.

26 Ibid., p. 343.

27 Bartram, *William Bartram on the Southeastern Indians*, p. 143, 127.

28 Wright, *The McGillivray & McIntosh Traders*, p. 52.

29 Saunt, *A New Order of Things*, p. 26.

30 Wright, *The McGillivray & McIntosh Traders*, p. 67.

31 Corkran, *The Creek Frontier, 1540-1783*, p. 26.

32 Caughey, *McGillivray of the Creeks*, p. 12.

33 Ibid., p. 3.

34 Wright, *The McGillivray and McIntosh Traders*, p. 85.

35 *Charleston (S.C.) Gazette*, (Massachusetts Spy), 9/30/1790.

36 Saunt, *A New Order of Things*, p. 67.

37 Pickett, *History of Alabama*, p. 343.

38 Cashin, *Lachlan McGillivray, Indian Trader*, p. 204.

39 Caughey, *McGillivray of the Creeks*, p. 16.

40 Wright, *The McGilliray and McIntosh Traders*, p 109.

41 Saunt, *A New Order of Things*, p. 21.

42 Green, *Alexander McGillivray*, p. 42.

43 Ibid., p. 41.

44 Pickett, *History of Alabama*, p. 431-432.

45 Saunt, *A New Order of Things*, p. 45.

46 Wright, *The McGillivray and McIntosh Traders*, p. 222.

47 Ethridge, *Creek Country*, p. 79.

48 Saunt, *A New Order of Things*, p. 70.

49 Ibid., p. 54.

50 Bartram, *The Travels of William Bartram*, p. 380, 393.

51 Pickett, *History of Alabama*, p. 87.

52 Angela Pulley Hudson, *Creek Paths and Federal Roads, Indians, Settlers, and Slaves and the Making of the American South*, (The University of North Carolina Press, Chapel Hill, 2010), p. 13.

53 Ibid., p. 47-48, 230, 62, 135.

54 Ibid., p. 56.

55 Ibid., p. 36.

56 Saunt, *A New Order of Things,* p. 40-41.

57 Ethridge, *Creek Country,* p. 128, 158.

58 Alan Gallay, *Colonial Wars of North America, 1512-1763,* Routledge Revivals: An Encyclopedia, 2015), p. 192.

59 Bartram, *William Bartram on the Southeastern Indians,* p. 118.

60 William Warren Rogers, Robert David Ward, Leah Rawls Atkins, and Wayne Flynt, *Alabama: The History of a Deep South State,* Bicentennial Edition, (The University of Alabama Press, Tuscaloosa, 2018), p. 15.

61 Ethridge, *Creek Country,* p. 98.

62 Rogers, *Alabama: The History of a Deep South State*, p. 14.

63 George Stiggins, *Creek Indian history: a historical narrative of the genealogy, traditions, and downfall of the Ispocoga or Creek Indian tribe of Indians, (Birmingham Public Library Press)*, p. 54

64 Bartram, *William Bartram on the Southeastern Indians,* p 16.

65 Corkran, *The Creek Frontier, 1540-1783*, p. 36.

66 Ibid., p. 39-40.

67 Hudson, *Creek Paths and Federal Roads – Indians, Settlers, and Slaves and the Making of the American South*, p. 20.

68 Bartram, *The Travels of William Bartram,* p. 40.

69 Saunt, *A New Order of Things,* p. 70.

70 Ethridge, *Creek Country*, p. 62.

71 Bartram, *The Travels of William Bartram,* p. 400, 403.

72 Bartram, *William Bartram on the Southeastern Indians,* p. 118.

73 Saunt, *A New Order of Things,* p. 23.

74 Ibid., p. 25.

75 Ibid., p. 33-34.

Chapter 2

76 Corkran, *The Creek Frontier,* p. 309.

77 Pickett, *History of Alabama,* p. 342.

78 http:///www.encyclopediaofAlabama.org. Jacob F.B. Lowrey, *David Taitt, (*accessed April 3, 2018*).*

79 Corkran, *The Creek Frontier,* p. 293.

80 Wright, *The McGillivray and McIntosh Traders,* p. 222.

81 Corkran, *The Creek Frontier,* p. 308.

82 Green, *Alexander McGilliray,* p. 45.

83 Saunt, *A New Order of Things,* p. 47.

84 Milfort, *Milfort's Memoirs,* Chapter 39.

85 Ibid., Chapter 38.

86 Ibid., Chapter 40.

87 Ibid., Chapter 4.

88 Ibid., Chapter 5.

89 Ibid., Chapter 6.

90 Ibid., Chapter 7.

91 Ibid., Chapter 9.

92 Ibid., Chapter 15.

93 Ibid., Chapter 44.

94 Ibid., Chapter 7.

95 Ibid., Chapter 41.

96 Ibid., Chapter 8.

97 Saunt, *A New Order of Things,* p. 16-17.

98 Milfort, *Milfort's Memoirs,* Chapter 22.

99 Colin G. Calloway, *The Indian World of George Washington,* (Oxford University Press, New York, New York, 2018), p. 350.

100 Kenneth Coleman, general editor, *A History of Georgia (The University of Georgia Press,* Athens, Georgia, 1977), p. 106.

101 Ibid., p. 92

102 Caughey, *McGillivray of the Creeks,* p. 73.

103 Milfort, *Milfort's Memoirs,* Chapter 40.

104 Ibid., Chapter 9.

105 Ibid., Chapter 9.

106 Ibid., Chapter 43.

107 Spencer C. Tucker, *Encyclopedia of North American Indian Wars, 1607-1890, A Political, Social and Military History,* ABC-CLIO, 2011), p. 259.

108 Milfort, *Milfort's Memoirs,* Chapter 23.

Chapter 3

109 Saunt, *A New Order of Things,* p. 84-85.

110 Joseph J. Ellis, "The McGillivray Moment," *I Wish I'd been there: twenty historians bring to life dramatic events that changed America,* edited by Byron Hollinshead, (Doubleday, New York, 2006), p. 53.

111 Pickett, *History of Alabama,* p. 366.

112 Caughey, *McGillivray of the Creeks,* p. 70.

113 Ibid., p. 62.

114 Corkran, *The Creek Frontier, 1540-1783*, p. 324.

115 Green, *Alexander McGillivray*, p. 46.

116 Pickett, *History of Alabama*, p. 366.

117 Green, *Alexander McGillivray*, p. 47.

118 Cotterill, *The Southern Indians*, p. 62.

119 Pickett, *History of Alabama*, p. 368.

120 Calloway, *The Indian World of George Washington*, p. 351; Pickett, *History of Alabama*, p. 368.

121 Caughey, *McGillivray of the Creeks*, p. 77.

122 Green, *Alexander McGillivray*, p. 48.

123 Caughey, *McGillivray of the Creeks*, p. 24.

124 Wright, *The McGillivray and McIntosh Traders*, p. 222.

125 Pickett, *History of Alabama*, p. 395.

126 Saunt, *A New Order of Things*, p. 75-76.

127 Green, *Alexander McGillivray*, p. 49.

128 Ibid., p. 51-52.

129 Ibid., p. 47-48.

130 Caughey, *McGillivray of the Creeks*, p. 71.

131 Pickett, *History of Alabama*, p. 368.

132 Caughey, *McGillivray of the Creeks*, p. 66.

133 Green, *Alexander McGillivray*, p. 51.

134 Joseph J. Ellis, *American Creation: Triumphs and Tragedies at the Founding of the Republic*, (Vintage Books, 2008), p 133, 135.

135 Pickett, *History of Alabama*, p. 369.

136 Caughey, *McGillivray of the Creeks*, P. 98.

137 Merritt B. Pound, *Benjamin Hawkins Indian Agent, (The University of Georgia Press, Athens,1951)*, p. 41.

138 Ibid., p. 44.

139 Ibid., p. 44.

140 Pickett, *History of Alabama*, p. 372.

141 Caughey, *McGillivray of the Creeks*, p. 103.

142 Pound, *Benjamin Hawkins*, p. 42

143 Pickett, *History of Alabama*, p. 374.

144 Caughey, *McGillivray of the Creeks*, p. 103-104.

145 Pickett, *History of Alabama*, p. 374.

146 Caughey, *McGillivray of the Creeks*, p. 90

147 Green, *Alexander McGillivray*, p. 52.

148 Ibid., p. 53.

149 Caughey, *McGillivray of the Creeks*, p. 93

150 Pound, *Benjamin Hawkins*, p. 55.

151 Caughey, *McGillivray of the Creeks*, p. 32.

152 Saunt, *A New Order of Things*, p. 83

153 Caughey, *McGillivray of the Creeks*, p. 32-33.

154 Wright, *The McGillivray and McIntosh Traders*, p. 223.

155 Pickett, *History of Alabama*, p. 383.

156 Ibid., p. 224.

157 Wright, *The McGillivray and McIntosh Traders*, p. 235.

158 Pound, *Benjamin Hawkins,* p. 55.

159 Benjamin Hawkins, *The Collected Works of Benjamin Hawkins, 1796-1810,* (University of Alabama Press, 2003), p. 55.

160 R. S. Cotterill, *The Southern Indians; The Story of the Civilized Tribes Before Removal,* (University of Oklahoma Press, 1954), p. 77.

Chapter 4

161 Joseph J. Ellis, *His Excellency George Washington,* (Vintage Books, A Division of Random House, Inc., 2004), p. 3.

162 Ibid., p. 6.

163 Ibid., p. 22

164 Ibid., p. 24.

165 Ellis, *American Creation,* p. 137.

166 Ibid., p. 36.

167 Mark Puls, *Henry Knox, Visionary General of the American Revolution,* (Palgrave MacMillan, 2008), p. 1-2, 4.

168 Ibid., p. 6.

169 Ibid., p. 21, 25.

170 Ibid., P. 28.

171 Ibid., p. 34.

172 http://www.Fortticonderoga.org. *Henry Knox and His Big Guns at Fort Ticonderoga,* (accessed April 14, 2018).

173 Ibid., p. 2.

174 Puls, *Henry Knox,* p. 38-39, 41.

175 Ibid., p. 45.

176 Ellis, *American Creation*, p. 88.

177 Ibid., p. 90-91.

178 Ibid., p. 99.

179 Ibid., p. 108.

180 Ibid., p. 112.

181 Ibid., p. 126.

182 Caughey, *McGillivray of the Creeks,* p. 200.

183 Calloway, *The Indian World of George Washington,* p. 356.

184 Ibid., p. 239.

185 Ibid., p. 36.

186 Ibid., p. 37.

187 http://www.moutvernon.org/reseach-collections/digital.encyclopedia/article/native-american-policy. George Washington's Mount Vernon, *Native American Policy,* (accessed March 5, 2015).

188 Caughey, *McGillivray of the Creeks,* p. 38.

189 W.W. Abbot, editor; Dorothy Twohig, associate editor, *The Papers of George Washington; Presidential Series,* (University of Virginia Press, 1987), Vol. 3, p. 139.

190 http://www.moutvernon.org/reseach-collections/digital.encyclopedia/article/native-american-policy. George Washington's Mount Vernon, *Native American Policy,* (accessed March 5, 2015).

191 Ellis, *American Creation,* p. 147.

192 Ibid., p. 132.

193 William Marinus Willett, *A Narrative of the Military Actions of Colonel Marinus Willett: Taken Chiefly from His Own Manuscript,* (G. & C. & H. Carvill, 1831), p. 94.

194 Ellis, *American Creation,* p. 137.

195 Ibid., p. 128.

196 Ellis, "The McGillivray Moment," p. 54.

197 Ellis, *American Creation,* p. 137.

198 Ellis, "The McGillivray Moment," p. 53.

199 Ellis, *American Creation,* p. 128,

200 "To George Washington from Henry Knox, 6 July 1789," *Founders Online,* National Archives, last modified February 21, 2017, http://www.foundersarchives.gov/documents/Washington/05-03-02-0062, (accessed March 5, 2015).

201 W.W. Abbot, *The Papers of George Washington*, Vol. 2, p. 491.

202 Ibid., p. 494.

203 "To George Washington from Henry Knox, 6 July 1789," *Founders Online,* National Archives, last modified February 21, 2017, http://www.foundersarchives.gov/documents/Washington/05-03-02-0062, (accessed March 5, 2015).

204 Abbot, *The Papers of George Washington,* Vol., 3, p. 134.

205 Ibid., p. 135.

206 Ibid., p. 137.

207 Ibid., p. 138-139.

208 Ellis, *American Creation,* p. 140.

209 De Pauw, Linda Grant, editor, *Documentary History of the First Federal Congress of the United States of America*, (The Johns Hopkins University Press, Baltimore and London, 1974), Vol. II, p. 31–35.

210 Bowling, Kenneth R. and Veit, Helen E., editors, *Documentary History of the First Federal Congress, The Diary of William Maclay and Other Notes on Senate Debates*, Vol. IX, p. 130-131.

211 Caughey, *McGillivray of the Creeks*, p. 39.

212 Ellis, *American Creation*, p. 149.

Chapter 5

213 Abbot, *The Papers of George Washington*, footnote to Knox February 15, 1790 letter, p. 144.

214 Ellis, *American Creation*, p. 150.

215 www.wikipedia.org, Henry Knox, Native American diplomacy and war, (accessed January 26, 2019).

216 Caughey, *McGillivray of the Creeks*, p. 243.

217 Ibid., p. 244.

218 Picketts, *History of Alabama*, p. 392.

219 Ibid., p. 394.

220 Ellis, *American Creation*, p. 142.

221 Willett, *A Narrative*, p. 95.

222 Caughey, *McGillivray of the Creeks*, p. 254

223 Abbot, *The Papers of George Washington*, Humphreys to Washington letter Sept. 26, 1789.

224 Caughey, *McGillivray of the Creeks.*, p. 260.

225 Picketts, *History of Alabama,* p. 397.

226 Pound, Merritt Blood, *Benjamin Hawkins Indian Agent,* (University of Georgia Press, Athens, 1951). p. 56.

227 Picketts, *History of Alabama,* p. 397-398.

228 Caughey, *McGillivray of the Creeks,* p. 251.

229 Ibid., p. 252-253.

230 Calloway, *The Indian World of George Washington,* p. 362.

231 Caughey, *McGillivray of the Creeks,* p. 253.

232 Abbot, *The Papers of George Washington, Rock Landing Sept. 27, 1789.*

233 *Salem Mercury,* Nov. 24, 1789.

234 Hawkins, *Indian Agent,* p. 196.

235 Ellis, *American Creation,* p. 133.

236 Abbott, *The Papers of George Washington,* Vol. 4, p. 472-473.

Chapter 6

237 Pound, *Benjamin Hawkins,* p. 52.

238 Abbot and Twohig, *The Papers of George Washington,* February 1790, vol. 5, p. 140.

239 Ibid., p. 141-142.

240 Ibid., p. 143.

241 Pound, *Benjamin Hawkins,* p. 57.

242 Pickett, *History of Alabama,* p. 399.

243 Caughey, *McGillivray of the Creeks,* p. 257-258.

244 Willett, *A Narrative,* p. 96.

Chapter 7

245 Pickett, *History of Alabama,* p. 400.

246 Willett, *A Narrative,* p. 97.

247 Pickett, *History of Alabama,* p. 400; Willett, *A Narrative,* p. 97.

248 Willett, *A Narrative,* p. 97.

249 Pickett, *History of Alabama,* p. 400.

250 Willett, *A Narrative,* p. 99.

251 Ibid., p. 101.

252 Ibid., p. 103.

253 Caughey, *McGilllivray of the Creeks,* p. 260-261.

254 Willett, *A Narrative,* p. 103.

255 Ibid., p. 105.

256 Pickett, *History of Alabama,* p. 402.

257 Willett, *A Narrative,* p. 105.

258 Ibid., 106-107.

259 Ibid., p 108-110.

Chapter 8

260 Caughey, *McGillivray of the Creeks,* p. 262.

261 Ibid., p. 270-271.

262 Caughey, *McGillivray of the Creeks,* p. 263.

263 *The New York Weekly Museum,* 6-12-1790, Issue 109, p. 3.

264 *New York Daily Gazette,* July 22, 1790.

265 Caughey, *McGillivray of the Creeks,* p. 263.

266 Willett, *A Narrative,* p. 113 footnote.

267 Ibid., p. 110

268 *New York Daily Gazette,* New York Public Library, 07-12-1790, Issue: 481: p. 658.

269 Willett, *A Narrative,* p. 111.

270 Willett, *A Narrative,* p. 111.

271 Ellis, *American Creation,* p. 151.

272 Willett, *A Narrative,* p. 111.

273 *The Federal Gazette,* Philadelphia Pennsylvania, New York Public Library, July 19, 1790, p.2.

274 Willett, *A Narrative,* p. 112.

275 *The Federal Gazette,* Residence Bill, July 17, 1790.

276 *New-York Daily Gazette,* New York, New York Public Library, July 22, 1790, Issue 490, p. 695.

277 *Maryland Journal,* Baltimore, Maryland, July 30, 1790, Vol. XVII; Issue 61; p. 2.

278 Ibid., p. 2.

279 *New-York Daily Gazette,* New York, New York, New York Public Library, July 22, *1790,* Issue 490, p. 695.

280 Saunt, *A New Order of Things,* p. 75.

281 *New-York Daily Gazette,* July 23, 1790, Issue 517, p. 802.

Chapter 9

282 Caughey, *McGillivray of the Creeks,* p. 43.

283 Ibid., p. 273.

284 Ellis, "The McGillivray Moment," p. 60

285 Abbot and Twohig, *The Papers of George Washington*, Vol 6, August 4, 1790, p. 189.

286 Ellis, "The McGillivray Moment," p. 57.

287 Ellis, *American Creation*, p. 153.

288 Caughey, *McGillivray of the Creeks*, p. 43.

289 Abbot and Twohig, *The Papers of George Washington*, Vol. 6, July 1790, p. 194- 195.

290 Ellis, "The McGillivray Moment," p. 57.

291 Pickett, *History of Alabama*, p. 405.

292 Caughey, *McGillivray of the Creeks*, p. 276.

293 Ibid., p. 277.

294 Abbot and Twohig, *The Papers of George Washington*, Vol. 6, July 1790, p. 102.

295 Pickett, *History of Alabama*, p. 405.

296 Caughey, *McGillivray of the Creeks*, p. 273

297 Ibid., p. 274.

298 Ibid., p. 44.

299 Ibid., p. 44.

300 Abbot and Twohig, *The Papers of George Washington*, Vol. 6, July 1790, p. 191.

301 Caughey, *McGillivray of the Creeks*, p. 274.

302 Abbot and Twohig, *The Papers of George Washington*, p. 195-196.

303 Caughey, *McGillivray of the Creeks*, p. 274.

304 "From George Washington to the United States Senate, 6 August 1790," http://www.founders.archives.gov. (accessed January 25, 2018).

305 Abbot and Twohig, *The Papers of George Washington,* Vol. 6, p. 212.

306 Ibid., p. 212.

307 Ibid., p. 212

308 "To George Washington from Henry Knox, 7 August 1790," http://www.founders.archives.gov. (accessed January 25, 2018).

309 Abbot and Twohig, *The Papers of George Washington,* Vol. 6, August 7 1790, p. 213.

310 Ibid., p. 251.

311 Ellis, *American Creation,* p. 156.

312 Abbot and Twohig, *The Papers of George Washington,* Vol. 6, p. 253.

313 Caughey, *McGillivray of the Creeks,* p. 273-275

314 Ibid., p. 276.

315 Ibid., p. 277.

316 Abbot and Twohig, *The Papers of George Washington*, Vol. 6. footnote 4, p. 214.

317 "Proclamation, 14 August 1790," *Founders Online,* National Archives, version of January 18, 2019, https://founders.archives.gov/documents/Washington/05-06-02-0122. Original source: *The Papers of George Washington,* Presidential Series, vol. 6, 1 July 1790 – 30 November 1790, ed. Mark A Mastromarino Charlottesville: University Press of Virginia, 1996, pp. 248 – 254, (accessed January 25, 2018).

318 Ibid.

319 Ellis, *American Creation*, p. 158.

320 Caughey, *McGillivray of the Creeks,* p. 278.

321 Calloway, *The Indian World of George Washington,* p. 373.

322 http://www.wardepartmentpapers.org. Papers of the War Department: 1784-1800, (accessed January 25, 2018).

323 Caughey, *McGillivray of the Creeks,* p. 279.

324 Ellis, "The McGillivray Moment," p. 57.

325 Caughey, *McGillivray of the Creeks,* p. 283.

326 Ibid., p. 280

327 Ibid., p. 44.

Chapter 10

328 Caughey, *McGillivray of the Creeks,* p. 279.

329 Ibid., p. 280.

330 Ibid., p. 283-284.

331 Ibid., p. 285.

332 Ibid., p. 45.

333 Abbot and Twohig, *The Papers of George Washington,* Vol. 6, August 1790, p. 215.

334 Ellis, "The McGillivray Moment," p. 61.

335 Ellis, *American Creation,* p. 159.

336 Caughey, *McGilllivray of the Creeks.*, p. 289.

337 Ibid., p. 290.

338 Ibid., p. 291.

339 Hawkins, Benjamin, *The Collected Works of Benjamin Hawkins, 1796-1810,* (University of Alabama Press, Tuscaloosa), p. 196.

340 http://wardepartmenetpapers.org. Papers of the War Department: 1784-1800, (accessed January 25, 2018).

341 Pickett, *History of Alabama*, p. 410.

342 *New York Daily Gazette,* p. 392, 396.

343 Caughey, *McGillivray of the Creeks, p. 299.*

344 Milfort, *Memoirs,* Chapter 20.

345 Caughey, *McGillivray of the Creeks*, p. 300.

346 Saunt, *A New Order of Things,* p. 87.

347 Abbott and Twohig, *The Papers of George Washington Presidential Series,* Vol. 8, p. 49.

348 Ellis, *His Excellency George Washington,* p. 214.

349 Abbott and Twohig, *The Papers of George Washington Presidential Series*, Vol. 8, p. 58-59.

350 Ellis, *American Creation,* p. 159.

351 Ibid., p. 162.

352 Pickett, *History of Alabama,* p. 413

353 John Pope, *A Tour Through the Southern and Western Territories of the United Sates of North-America.,* (Charles L. Woodward, 1888), p. 48.

354 http://wardepartmenetpapers.org. Papers of the War Department: 1784-1800, (accessed January 25, 2018).

355 http://wardepartmenetpapers.org. Papers of the War Department: 1784-1800, (accessed January 25, 2018).

356 Caughey, *McGillivray of the Creeks,* p. 347.

357 Milfort, *Memoirs,* chapter 25.

358 Ibid., p. 46-47.

359 Ellis, *American Creation,* p. 160.

360 Caughey, *McGillivray of the Creeks*, p. 301-302.

361 Ibid., p. 304.

362 Ibid., p. 308-309.

363 Ibid., p. 288.

364 Ibid., p. 50.

365 Ibid., p. 318.

366 Ibid., p. 51.

367 Pickett, *History of Alabama,* p. 414.

368 Caughey, *McGillivray of the Creeks,* p. 329.

369 Ibid., p. 322, 328.

370 Ibid., p 323-324.

371 Pound, Merritt, *Benjamin Hawkins, Indian Agent,* (University of Georgia Press, Athens, 1951), p. 197.

372 Caughey, *McGillivray of the Creeks*, p. 329-330.

373 Calloway, *The Indian World of George Washington,* p. 375.

374 Pickett, *History of Alabama,* p. 429.

375 Caughey, *McGillivray of the Creeks* p. 348.

376 Ibid., p. 350.

377 Ibid., p. 353.

378 Ibid.,, p. 354.

379 Pickett, *History of Alabama,* p. 431.

380 Wright, *The McGillivray and McIntosh Traders,* p. 250.

381 Ibid., p. 247-248.

382 Ibid., p. 248.

383 Caughey, *McGillivray of the Creeks,* p. 362.

384 http://infoweb.newsbank.com/iw-search/we/HistARchive/?p_product=EANX, *The Washington Spy,* June 13, 1792, Issue 103, p.3, (accessed April 4, 2014).

385 Pickett, *History of Alabama,* p. 430.

386 Wright, *The McGillivray and McIntosh Traders,* p. 254.

387 Pickett, *History of Alabama,* p. 431-432.

388 Ibid., p. 75 footnote.

389 Ibid., p. 414.

390 Elllis, *American Creation,* p. 161.

391 Elllis, *His Excellency,* p. 238.

BIBLIOGRAPHY

Abbot, W.W., editor; Dorothy Twohig, associate editor. *The Papers of George Washington; Presidential Series*, Charlottesville: University of Virginia Press, 1987.

"Alexander McGillivray (ca. 1750-1793)." Accessed August 4, 2013. http://www.georgiaencyclopedia.org/nge/ArticlePrintable.jsp?id=h-690.

American Society for Ethnohistory. *Four Centuries of Southern Indians*. Athens: University of Georgia Press, 1975.

"Augusta." *The New York Weekly Museum*, June 12, 1790.

"Authentic Intelligence of Fresh Disturbances among the Creek Indians." *Maryland Journal*, December 9, 1791.

Bartram, William. *The Travels of William Bartram*. New York: Dover Publications, 1955.

Bartram, William. *William Bartram on the Southeastern Indians*. Indians of the Southeast. Lincoln: University of Nebraska Press, 1995.

"By Authority (GW Announcement of Treaty)." *The Gazette of the United States*, August 14, 1790.

Calloway, Colin G. *The Indian World of George Washington*. New York: Oxford University Press, 2018.

Cashin, Edward J. *Lachlan McGillivray, Indian Trader: The Shaping of the Southern Colonial Frontier*. Athens: University of Georgia Press, 1992.

Caughey, John Walton, and University of South Carolina. *McGillivray of the Creeks*. Southern Classics Series. Columbia: University of South Carolina Press in cooperation with the Institute for Southern Studies of the University of South Carolina, 2007.

Center for History and New Media. "Zotero Quick Start Guide," n.d. http://zotero.org/support/quick_start_guide.

"Col. Mcgillivray; Creeks; New Orleans." *Gazette of the United States*, October 13, 1792.

Coleman, Kenneth. General Editor, *A History of Georgia,* Second Edition. Athens: University of Georgia Press, 1991.

Columbian Centinel. July 24, 1790.

Corkran, David H. *The Creek Frontier, 1540-1783*. 1st ed. Civilization of the American Indian Series, v. 86. Norman: University of Oklahoma Press, 1967.

Cotterill, R. S. *The Southern Indians; the Story of the Civilized Tribes before Removal.* 1st ed. The Civilization of the American Indian 38. Norman: University of Oklahoma Press, 1954.

"Creek Confederacy and a Sketch of the Creek Country" Accessed September 25, 2013. http://archive.org/stream/creekconfederacy00hawk#page/n3/mode/2up.

"Death Notice." *Washington Spy*, June 13, 1792.

Edmunds, R. David. *Studies in Diversity American Indian Leaders.* Lincoln and London: University of Nebraska Press, 1980.

Ellis, Joseph J. *American Creation: Triumphs and Tragedies at the Founding of the Republic.* New York: Vintage Books, 2008.

Ellis, Joseph J. *His Excellency George Washington*. New York: Vintage Books, 2005.

Ellis, Joseph J. "The McGillivray Moment," *I Wish I'd Been There*, edited by Byron Hollinshead. New York, London, Toronto, Sydney, Auckland: Doubleday, 2006.

"Encyclopedia of Alabama: David Taitt." Accessed September 9, 2013. http://www.encyclopediaofalabama.org/face/Article.jsp?id=h-1538.

Essex Journal, November 18, 1789.

Ethridge, Robbie Franklyn. *Creek Country: The Creek Indians and Their World*. Chapel Hill: University of North Carolina Press, 2003.

"Extract Fom Gov Telrair's Address to Both Houses of the Legislature." *New York Daily Gazette*, July 12, 1790.

"Extract of a Letter from a Gentleman in Nashville, to His Friend in His Town." *Washington Spy*, October 25, 1788.

"For the New-York Daily Gazette." *New-York Daily Gazette*, August 24, 1790.

Frank, Andrew. *Creeks and Southerners*. Lincoln: University of Nebraska Press, 2005.

"From the Charleston (S.C.) Gazette." *Massachusetts Spy*, September 30, 1790.

"Full Text of Archives of Aboriginal Knowledge. Containing All the Original Paper Laid before Congress Respecting the History, Antiquities, Language, Ethnology, Pictography, Rites, Superstitions, and Mythology, of the Indian Tribes of the United States.'" Accessed September 23, 2013.

http://www.archive.org/stream/archivesknow05schorich/archiv
esknow05schorich_djvu.txt.

"Gen. Alexander McGilllivray." *Gazette of the United States*,
June 1, 1793.

George Washington. "Index to Washington References to
AM." Accessed August 4, 2013. http://memory.loc.gov/cgi-
bin/query.

"Georgetown, November 25. Extract of a Letter from St.
Augustine." *Norwich Packet*, December 25, 1789.

"Georgia Gazette." *Georgia Gazette*, June 10, 1790.

"Gray's Ferry, July 17, 1790." *The Federal Gazette and
Philadelphia Daily Advertiser*, July 17, 1790.

Green, Donald Edward. *The Creek People*. Phoenix Ariz.:
Indian Tribal Series, 1973.

Green, Michael D. "Alexander McGillivray," *Studies in
Diversity American Indian Leaders,* edited by R. David
Edmunds, Lincoln and London, University of Nebraska Press,
1980.

Hahn, Steven C. *The Invention of the Creek Nation, 1670-1763*.
U of Nebraska Press, 2004.

Hawkins, Benjamin. *The Collected Works of Benjamin Hawkins,
1796-1810*. Tuscaloosa: University of Alabama Press, 2003.

Hollinshead, Byron, ed. *I Wish I'd Been There: Twenty
Historians Bring to Life Dramatic Events That Changed America*.
1st ed. New York: Doubleday, 2006.

Hudson, Angela Pulley. *Creek Paths and Federal Roads —
Indians, Settlers, and Slaves and the Making of the American
South*. Chapel Hill: The University of North Carolina Press,
2010.

"JSTOR: The Georgia Historical Quarterly, Vol. 51, No. 4 (December, 1967), p. 379-400." Accessed August 10, 2013. http://www.jstor.org/discover/10.2307/40578728?uid=3739520&uid=2129&uid=2134&uid=2473443307&uid=2&uid=70&uid=3&uid=2473443297&uid=3739256&uid=60&purchase-type=both&accessType=none&sid=21102541651067&showMyJstorPss=false&seq=2&showAccess=false.

Knox, Henry. "Letter to George Washington from Henry Knox," July 7, 1789.

"Regarding Treaty of New York between Creeks and United States." http://wardepartmentpapers.org/document.php?id=4595, August 20, 1790. http://wardepartmentpapers.org/document.php?id=4595.

"List Of Creek Towns." Accessed September 8, 2013. http://www.accessgenealogy.com/native/creek/migration/list_of_creek_towns.htm.

Martin, Joel W. *Sacred Revolt: The Muskogees' Struggle for a New World*. Boston: Beacon Press, 1991.

Maryland Journal, July 30, 1790.

Massachusetts Spy, November 11, 1788.

"Milfort's Memoirs Introduction & Contents." Accessed September 10, 2013. http://homepages.rootsweb.ancestry.com/~cmamcrk4/mlfrttoc.html.

New York Daily Gazette, July 3, 1790.

New York Daily Gazette, July 21, 1790.

New York Daily Gazette, July 22, 1790.

New York Daily Gazette, August 14, 1790.

New York Daily Gazette, August 23, 1790.

"Our Georgia History (Go to Website to Verify)." Accessed September 8, 2013. http://www.ourgeorgiahistory.com/indians/Creek/creek01.html .

"Philadelphia July 19." *Federal Gazette*, July 19, 1790.

Pickett, Albert James. *History of Alabama*. Montgomery AL: River City Publishing, 2003.

Pope, John. *A Tour Through the Southern and Western Territories of the United States of North-America: The Spanish Dominions on the River Mississippi, and the Floridas; the Countries of the Creek Nations; and Many Uninhabited Parts*. Charles L. Woodward, 1888.

Pound, Merritt Bloodworth. *Benjamin Hawkins, Indian Agent*. Athens: University of Georgia Press, 1951.

Rogers, William Warren; Ward, Robert David; Atkins, Leah Rawls; Flynt, Wayne. *Alabama The History of a Deep South State*. Tuscaloosa: The University of Alabama Press, 1994.

Rough Sketches of the Creek Country (Alabama, n.d. http://memory.loc.gov/cgi-bin/query/D?gmd:1:./temp/~ammem_MznM::@@@mdb.

Salem Mercury, November 24, 1789.

Saunt, Claudio. *A New Order of Things: Property, Power, and the Transformation of the Creek Indians, 1733-1816*. Cambridge Studies in North American Indian History. Cambridge; New York: Cambridge University Press, 1999.

"Secret Articles of US/Creek Treaty of 07/04/1790." http://wardepartmentpapers.org/document.php?id=4564,

August 7, 1790.
http://wardepartmentpapers.org/document.php?id=4564.

Stiggins, George. *Creek Indian History: A Historical Narrative of the Genealogy, Traditions, and Downfall of the Ispocoga or Creek Indian Tribe of Indians.* Birmingham, Ala: Birmingham Public Library Press, 1989.

"The Avalon Project: Treaty With the Creeks: 1790." Text. Accessed August 10, 2013.
http://avalon.law.yale.edu/18th_century/cre1790.asp.

"Travels in the American Colonies, Ed. under the Auspices of the National Society of the Colonial Dames of America, by Newton D. Mereness." Accessed September 9, 2013.
http://memory.loc.gov/cgi-bin/query/h?ammem/lhbtnbib:@field(NUMBER+@band(lhbtn+09410)).

"Treaty Signed." *New York Daily Gazette*, n.d.

Washington, George. "Washington Letter to Henry Knox," March 8, 1790.
http://memory.loc.gov/mss/mgw/mgw2/035/1220111.jpg.

Willett, William Marinus. *A Narrative of the Military Actions of Colonel Marinus Willett: Taken Chiefly from His Own Manuscript.* G. & C. & H. Carvill, 1831.

Wright, Amos. *The McGillivray and McIntosh Traders on the Old Southwest Frontier, 1716-1815.* Montgomery, Ala: NewSouth Books, 2001.

INDEX